OPEN TO REASON

by David L. Neuhouser

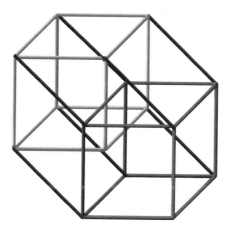

A Tesseract, or Hypercube: a symbol for the imagination.

"the wisdom from above is open to reason"
James 3:17

MURDOCK LEARNING RESOURCE CENTER
GEORGE FOX UNIVERSITY
NEWBERG, OR. 97132

Scripture quotations are from the following sources:

Authorized King James Version (KJV), 1611.

Revised Standard Version (RSV), 1611, 1881, 1901, 1946.

Scripture taken from the
HOLY BIBLE, NEW INTERNATIONAL VERSION.
Copyright © 1973, 1978, 1984 International Bible Society.
Used by permission of Zondervan Bible Publishers.

Published by Taylor University Press
236 West Reade Avenue
Upland, Indiana 46989

This book is dedicated
to Ruth.
I know
as a result of experience,
intuition, and reason,
that what her love
has done for me is beyond all
imagining.

TABLE OF CONTENTS

PREFACE

All aspects of human experience should be open to reason. Reason has a role to play in religion as well as in mathematics and science. Reason's role in religion has been greatly underrated by some and vastly overrated by others. The consequences of each error may be great. Those who underrate its contribution may be limiting their understanding of religion, perhaps getting out of touch with the truth, and certainly hindering their influence with those who refuse to turn off their minds when considering religion. Those who overrate its role usually do so because they really do not understand its role in mathematics and science. These people may eventually even give up on religion altogether because of demanding an unreasonable standard of proof resulting from their misunderstanding of mathematics and science. For these reasons, I want to share my conclusions as a professor of mathematics about the role of reason. These conclusions, although tentative, are the result of many years of study and prayer; and my hope is that this sharing of them will contribute to a continuing process of understanding the role of reason in religion.

The three parts of this book correspond to the three prayers in the song "Day by Day" from the musical Godspell.

"To see Thee more clearly,

To love Thee more dearly,

To follow Thee more nearly."

To see God more clearly is to know Him better and Part I is an examination of the relation between reason, faith, and knowledge. Part II is the relation between reason and love. To follow God more nearly is to obey Him and Part III is the relation between reason and obedience or Christian living. These three things (knowledge, love, and obedience) are closely related so the parts overlap. However, although reading the parts in the order given should contribute best to understanding the role of reason, each of the three parts may be read separately, Some may only be interested in one or two of the parts and so may prefer to read just those parts.

I believe that man is a unity, not an aggregate of disjointed parts. Hence, faith, reason, experience, love, obedience, and imagination are all interconnected and none of them can exist alone. Each of these ingredients, in proper relation to the others, contributes to our understanding of reality. And in every case, although the life-giving quality is not in reason, it is reason which must evaluate, make choices, and eventually govern. Therefore, the mathematician, scientist, theologian, philosopher, artist and poet must be concerned with all of these things. It is not the case that the mathematician is concerned only with reason, the scientist only with experience, the theologian only with faith, and the artist only with imagination. The differences in their work and thought processes lie in the relative proportions and emphases of these ingredients, so that, for example, the poet and the mathematician contribute to our understanding by using the same ingredients but in a different mix.

I have come to these conclusions primarily through my study of and activities in mathematics and Christianity. Science must enter into the discussions because of its very nature. Because of its close relation to mathematics, I have had a continuing interest in the nature and basic methods of science. History is an avocation of mine, so I have been interested in the history of mathematics, science, and Christianity. Another of my interests is literature, and I believe that literature contributes to our ability to see things from different points of view and so contributes to our understanding of almost everything.

The things I have to say are not original. I am indebted to all the authors of the many books I have read and my teachers, colleagues, students, and friends. The sources should be evident in most cases from the quotations and footnotes. Where credit is not given to someone else, it is still not correct to assume that finally there is an original contribution of mine. It simply means that I am not aware of the source. In my younger days, I often believed that certain of my "profound" views were my own thoughts. But, I usually found on the rereading of an old favorite book "my idea," even at times expressed in my own words! So, although the ideas themselves are not original with me, the responsibility for synthesis into this particular system or conglomeration must be borne by me.

The many quotations are a reminder of my indebtedness to others. They are used mainly because they express the thought I want to express and say it much better than I can. As one of Charles Williams' characters in _Shadows of Ecstasy_ said, I am not simply quoting, I am expressing my thought in their words. Of course, I can't deny that one reason for quoting is to use the weight of others opinions. I realize, and the reader should be aware, that the people quoted are responsible only for the words they used and not for any use or misuse to which I have put them. I do not claim that anyone quoted by me would agree with all that I have written. I could almost guarantee that none would agree with everything here. Neither do I claim to agree with everyone quoted on all other issues. All quotations from the Bible are from the Revised Standard Version unless otherwise noted.

I only hope that it is not quite true of me what a character in Lewis Carroll's book _Sylvie and Bruno_ said of another person in the story, "For utterly inappropriate and irrelevant quotations, you are 'ekalled by few and excelled by none!'"

I must express special gratitude for the writings of George MacDonald, C.S. Lewis, and Elton Trueblood. Lewis and Trueblood were particularly helpful to me at a time when I was having serious doubts about the reality of Christianity. In addition to the help that his books have been to me, Elton Trueblood gave me good advice and valuable encouragement after reading an early version of _Open to Reason_. All of them, and particularly MacDonald, have been a continuing source of strength and inspiration to me in my Christian life and in my intellectual life.

Many of these ideas came to me while studying for courses taught at Taylor University, particularly honors seminars on faith and learning and Biblical Literature II. The discussions with students and colleagues in these courses were helpful in clarifying my ideas. The discipline of trying to get them on paper has been most beneficial also. A sabbatical leave gave me time to write and this kind of writing is a discipline not well developed in me due to my activities in mathematics. I am thankful for the support and encouragement from Taylor University administrators, especially Steve Bedi. The excellent work of Dan Jordan, Roger Judd, and the staff at the University Press is much appreciated. I am also indebted to Jan King for help with typing and proof reading and especially to Roger Phillips and Heidi Morrow for eliminating errors in grammar, punctuation, and spelling and for improvement in clarity. The responsibility for any remaining errors and unclear passages is entirely mine.

I am most indebted to my wife. She is a constant support and source of strength in ways too numerous to mention. Anything that I do must be considered a cooperative endeavor with her. The ideas expressed in this book have been discussed with her over a period of many years. Conversations about these ideas with my children have been very helpful also.

Part I
Faith & Reason

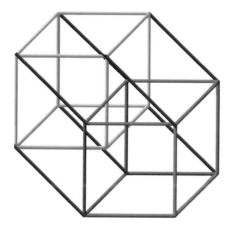

"It is fatal to let people suppose that Christianity is only a mode of feeling; it is vitally necessary to insist that it is first and foremost a rational explanation of the universe."

Dorothy Sayers

"My own approach to the problem of the reality of spirit has been much the same as a physicist in dealing with the reality of matter."

William Pollard

Introduction

"All is but a woven web of guesses."

Xenophones

In the short story "Pigeon Feathers," John Updike has made, I believe, a modern myth.[1] Following is my retelling of that myth. By chance, a boy reads in his father's book that there is no God. This startles the boy into really considering the question. Authorities in his life, parents, grandmother and pastor, cannot help him. So finally, one night while he is lying in bed, he reaches up his hands into the darkness and prays, "God, if there is a God, reach down and touch my hands." Then a wonderful thing happens. God gently touches his hands and the boy goes to sleep, satisfied. The next day he thinks about his experience and happily remembers how gently God touched him, ever so gently just the way a loving God would touch. It had been a soft touch, so soft that as he thinks about it, he wonders if it really happened at all. Maybe he only imagined it. And so he is right back where he started. There is more in Updike's story, but this is all I want to consider now.

This experience of the boy typifies the experience of many of us. We have an experience in which it is clear to us that God is acting in some real and positive way. But then, later, as we think back on the event we are not sure; maybe we only imagined it. There are always other possible explanations for whatever happened. Which is the truth?

The ancient Greek poet described the problem of knowing the truth in the following poem.

The Ethiops say that their gods are flat-nosed and black
While the Thracians say that theirs have blue eyes and red hair.

Yet if cattle or horses or lions had hands and could draw
And could sculpture like men, then the horses would draw their gods
Like horses, and the cattle like cattle, and each would then shape
Bodies of gods in the likeness, each kind, of its own.

The gods did not reveal, from the beginning,
All things to us; but in the course of time,
Through seeking, men find that which is the better...

These things are, we conjecture, like the truth.

But as for certain truth, no man has known it.
Nor will he know it; neither of the gods.
Nor yet of all the things of which I speak.
And even if by chance he were to utter
The final truth, he would himself not know it:
For all is but a woven web of guesses.[2]

Is there really any way of knowing the truth about religion? Is religious knowledge different from knowledge in other fields? Part of the problem is the lack of understanding of the interconnectedness of all areas of learning and the interconnectedness of all ways of knowing. It may be that a "woven web of guesses" could be quite strong indeed.

Many believe that mathematics involves only reason; science, only experience; and religion, only faith. In my experience, mathematics requires all three, and in addition a great deal of imagination. Science and religion require each of these also. One of the aims of Part I is to explore the roles of experience, imagination, faith, and especially, reason in mathematics, science and religion. I will not be considering religion in general, but Christianity in particular because Christianity is the religion in which my experience, imagination, and reason have led me to faith. A related objective is to discover the similarities in the methods of mathematics, science, and religion.

Another goal of this section on Faith and Reason is to destroy some misconceptions. Some people believe that certainty resides in mathematics and nowhere else. In earlier ages many mathematicians believed this. By looking at the historical development of mathematics we will be able to see why this view is incorrect. Others believe that in science experience will lead us to facts unsullied by theory. We will see that experience alone without reason, imagination, or faith is an impossibility. The idea that in religion knowledge comes only through revelation and faith must be wrong because, again, it is impossible to isolate these from experience, imagination, and reason.

Some Christians seem actually to be afraid of using reason in their religion. Why reason should be feared more than emotion or tradition is beyond my comprehension. And if reason is not allowed in religion, then other forces acting upon us (such as emotion, tradition, peer and culture pressure) are, correspondingly, more powerful. God gave us minds to use. It is true that because of the Fall our ability to think has been impaired; we are finite, so our ability to reason is limited. However, our feelings are subject at least as much to the same shortcomings.

Perfect love casts out all fear. Since God is perfect love, we do not need to fear anything. Without fear we are free to reason, which can be an aid to clarification in all areas of life. This fear some Christians have of reason not only cripples their own development but can be a stumbling block to those who do not believe.

The relationships we find between the so-called secular and the spiritual aspects of our lives point out the unity of all things and the integrity of God. God does not want us to be fragmented but to be whole.

Truth and Reality

"Truth is always <u>about</u> something,
but reality is that <u>about which</u> truth is."

C.S. Lewis

Truth might be defined as whatever does not disturb what we already believe. Unfortunately, this "definition" fairly accurately describes what most of us are willing to call truth, but it fails dismally to give an adequate conception of what truth really is.

"What is true for you may not be true for me," sounds true. But can this statement itself be true for me and not for you? "All truth is relative," is a logical contradiction. Either it is absolutely true, in which case not all truth is relative, or else it is false, which means some truths are not relative. In either case we have established the falsity of the statement, "All truth is relative." However, many people quote it. Somehow, it seems to be so true! We are getting into difficulty because we are using the words "true" or "truth" in discussing what truth is.

One philosopher, Elton Trueblood, discusses three theories of truth: pragmatism, coherence, and correspondence.[1] According to pragmatism, statements are true if they are useful. In the coherence theory, they are true if they are logically consistent with each other. The correspondence theory says that statements are true if they are in agreement with reality.

The correspondence theory is, I believe, what most common people mean when they use the word "true." It certainly is the way I use the term. Notice, however, that it implies the belief in an objective reality. Some deny the existence of an objective reality. According to Einstein, however, "The belief in an external world independent of the percipient subject is the foundation of all science."[2] Just because I believe in an objective reality, it does not mean that I believe that I can know all about that reality. So a distinction must be made between truth and knowledge. My knowledge may be relative, but it does not make sense to talk about knowledge at all if there is no reality.

Those who would argue that all reality is subjective, by the fact that they are arguing, are making a claim that their statements are true, in the sense of agreement with reality. In other words, it seems to me that it is a logical contradiction to claim that all reality is subjective. It is impossible for my mind to make sense out of a disbelief in an ultimate reality. What that ultimate reality *is* may be impossible for me to know, but that there *is* an ultimate reality I am firmly convinced. C. S. Lewis once said that "those people who don't believe in their own existence, nevertheless ask you, when at table, to pass them the salt. 'Where do they put it?'"[3]

You might claim, for example, that mathematics is boring, while I would insist that it is interesting. Does not that show that truth is relative? We had better clarify what we mean. The statement, "Mathematics is interesting to me," is true or false depending on who says it. That is, its truth depends on who says it. But, if we know who is saying it, then it must be either true or false.

If I had said that everyone finds mathematics interesting and you think it is dull, then you have proved that my statement is false, (not true) in that it is not in agreement with reality. If I make the more modest claim that some people find mathematics to be interesting, it may be true. But it is either true or false and not relatively true.

Consider the blind men who investigated an elephant by feeling it. One felt its leg and said, "An elephant is like a tree." Another felt its side and said that it is like a wall. Does this mean that truth is relative? No, it means that their knowledge is relative to, or dependent on, their experience. There is an ultimate reality, the elephant.. They may have partial truths: part of an elephant is like a wall, part of an elephant is like a tree.

When people say that Christianity may be true for you but not for me, they are probably using the pragmatic theory of truth. They mean that it may work for you but not for me. There are problems with this view. For example, what does it mean to say "it works" or "it is useful?" Useful for what? I might believe that I am under constant surveillance by the police. Every time I get in my car, they follow me, ready to arrest me if I violate any law. Now this belief might be useful if it causes me to drive carefully and not have an accident. With the pragmatic theory I could say it was true. However, it is false in that in reality, the police are not constantly watching me. If a statement is true, it is likely to be useful for something. But just because a statement may be useful does not mean it is true.

In the same way, if statements are true, they will be coherent or consistent. However, statements may be consistent without being true. A man may be a very good liar and come up with a consistent story even though it is not true. A law court often uses the coherence or consistency theory of truth. If a lawyer can catch a witness in an inconsistency, then they conclude that his testimony is false. On the other hand, if no inconsistencies are found, the witness might still be lying, but we cannot prove it.

There are also levels of truth. "Devotion to truth is not identical with the cult of facts."[4] A historian may know many true facts about the Civil War and yet not understand the truth about the war. Bruce Catton, perhaps the historian who knows most about the Civil War, has been asked, "Isn't there one good book that will give me an understanding of the war?" Catton says that after resisting the impulse to name five or six of his own books, he usually answers by saying, "Read *John Brown's Body* by Stephen Vincent Benet."[5] This long narrative poem communicates truth about the war at a deeper level than most large collections of isolated facts. For another example, many people knew facts about the moon's movement and falling bodies near the earth's surface, but Isaac Newton arrived at a much deeper truth through his laws of motion, the law of universal gravitation, and calculus.

There is another way in which the word "truth" is used which may cause some confusion. When what I say is in agreement with what I really believe even if it is not the truth, Samuel Johnson calls moral truth. Now what I believe may be, in fact, false, in which case it would be what Dr. Johnson calls a physical untruth. With this definition of moral truth, I might say the opposite of what you say but we are both speaking the truth. In this sense truth is relative, relative to what I believe and what you believe. But physical truth is not relative.

I believe, then, that statements, if they are meaningful, are either true or false. I may never know whether a statement is true or false, but its truth or falsity is not dependent on my knowledge. The problem of knowledge is the subject of the next chapter. But before we consider that difficult problem, I would like to call your attention to some views of religion which show the importance of the meaning of truth and reality.

The following quotation describes how some people view truth in relation to religion.

"Finally the question can be raised whether religion is the sort of thing that could be true. Perhaps it is a matter of taste, a matter of personal preference, a 'picture-preference,' as it has been called. Matters that are true or false are those in which there is some agreed method by which their truth may be established. The natural sciences have given our culture a staggeringly powerful model of how what is true and what is false can really be decided, because we have agreed to accept its method of settling such questions. But who can say how we should settle which of men's religions, if any, is true? And if we cannot agree on that, then surely religions are of preference or cultural conditioning, but the doctrines of religions seem immune from falsifications, as they are also immune from verification. In which case, truth is hardly at stake."[6]

At another point in the same book, the author states that it is a fact that saying a statement is true is actually just an assessment of its usefulness.[7] I believe that this is a dangerous, even insidious, and false view. The power and limitations of science will be discussed in a later chapter. Whether or not a particular religion can be verified or falsified in this life, has nothing to do with whether or not it is true, only whether or not it can be known to be true in this life. For example, Christianity claims that there is life after death. Surely, this claim is either in agreement with reality or not. It is not just a question of whether or not it seems to work for me.

Finally, I believe that it is important not only to understand the meaning of truth but also to desire to know the truth. "We must work very hard to restore first in ourselves and then, by influence in others, opposed to that 'furious pursuit of pleasure ending in actual desire of honor and delight in death,' the pursuit of truth, ending in actual desire of beauty and delight in life."[8]

Knowledge and Certainty

"Its better tew know nothing, than tew know what ain't so."

Josh Billings

What does it mean to say, "I know p," where p is any statement? Some statements that are similar, at least in form, are "I believe p," "It is my opinion that p," and "I feel p." I have asked students what they mean by these statements and have received many different answers. That is why we need to clarify how we are using the word "know," at least if we want to communicate with each other.

Is the difference between know, believe, and feel in the way we have arrived at p or in the degree of certainty we have in p or something else? Let's consider some hypothetical situations. Suppose that I say that I know "Team A beat Team B in basketball last night." However, when pressed, I have to admit that I did not see the game and I have not received any information about the game. I just have a feeling in my bones and am sure Team A did beat Team B last night. However, even if, in actual fact, Team A did beat Team B last night, you probably think I should not claim knowledge of that fact because I do not possess adequate evidence.

Now suppose that on a later occasion I claim, "Team C beat Team D last night." Also, knowing your desire for reasons for my claim, I add that I saw the score in the morning newspaper and a friend of mine who attended the game reported the same information to me. However, this time it turns out that Team C was defeated by Team D. My friend left the game with 25 seconds remaining in the game and Team C leading by eight points. But then, amazingly, Team D made three baskets from three point range. Furthermore, when I read the score in the paper, either there was a mistake in the paper or the information got garbled on entering my mind. Both of these things have actually happened to me. This time, you would probably object to my claim of knowledge on the basis that the statement was not true even though I seemed to have good evidence for it.

We have one more situation to consider and it is also hypothetical, I hope. Suppose that by now I am getting a little paranoid and although Team E defeats Team F and I have abundant evidence for that fact, I irrationally have a strong belief that the opposite is true. However, because of the evidence and your attitude, I feel that I must say that Team E beat Team F. A lie detector to which I am attached (now you understand why I am paranoid?) indicates that I am lying even though what I say is true and I have evidence that it is true. Again, we must say that it is incorrect for me to say "I know" in this case.

These three hypothetical situations illustrate what many philosophers consider to be the three conditions for knowledge of a statement p:

1. I believe p.
2. p is true.
3. I have adequate evidence for p.[1]

Of these three conditions, only the first is easy. I am usually fairly certain whether I believe something or not. The second condition is extremely difficult; some would say it is an impossible one. The third is also very difficult. There are many different ideas about what constitutes adequate evidence. And perhaps the worst part of this one is that each of us has different standards for various kinds of knowledge. That is, I probably demand more and different kinds of evidence in one area than I do in another. We will grapple with these problems throughout Part I of this book.

Epistemology is the theory of the origin, nature, methods, and limits of knowledge. Karl Popper, an eminent philosopher of science, has an interesting diagram to help us understand the difficulties in epistemology.[2] Figure 3-1 pictures three planes, labeled E, O and L. Plane E represents essential reality, the real world. A and B represent real events in plane E. Plane O represents observational reality, our sense impressions of the real world. a and b represent what our various senses tell us about events A and B. Plane L represents language, our symbolic representation of our observations. So α and β are our symbolic descriptions of a and b. Thus, according to this scheme, by the time we try to communicate our "knowledge" we are twice removed from essential reality.

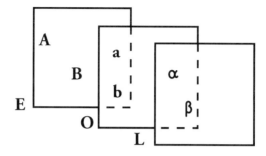

Figure 3-1.

To make it even worse, there are various kinds of filters between the planes. Between planes E and O there could be an emotional filter depending on the state of our emotions at the time of the events. Also, our world view is a filter between those planes. Our fundamental assumptions about the nature of the world determine, to a certain extent, what registers in our minds. Those facts that agree with our world view get through the filter much more easily than those at variance with our basic beliefs.

Fiction can sometimes pierce this filter. That is what C.S. Lewis meant when he said that an atheist must be very careful what he reads. For example, as a young atheist, Lewis read Phantastes by George MacDonald and Holiness pierced Lewis' filter; beginning a process which eventually led to the end of Lewis' atheism. Later as an author, Lewis believed that "any amount of theology could be smuggled into people's minds under cover of romance without their knowing it."[3] He thought that by means of science fiction or children's fairy tales he could slip through this filter, or as he put it, he could "steal past those watchful dragons."[4] In any case, if we really want to arrive at truth in essential reality, we need to be aware of this world view filter.

In Figure 3-1, there also should be a language or articulation filter between O and L. We may have trouble finding words (α and β) to express our sense impressions (a and b) of events (A and B). Then, if for any reason our symbolic description of an event is inadequate, we may allow this inadequate description to mislead us about the events. Thus our mind-set is determined more by our poor description than by the original sense impressions. Besides our skill, or lack of skill, in handling language, there is a difference in the degree to which one language can describe a certain type of event and that to which another language can describe the same event. For example, it has been said that Eskimos have many words for snow so that they can distinguish between the different kinds. Of course it is more important for them to be able to do that than it is for those who live in warmer climates. But if they did not have those language capabilities, their ability to distinguish between different aspects of weather might be more difficult. As another example, the Greeks had more than ten words for various kinds of love.[5]

In light of these difficulties, let us consider again the third condition for knowledge, that is, adequate evidence. What are the types of evidence we give? That is, what kinds of answers do we give when we are asked, "How do you know that?" I believe there are four categories into which our answers fall. Of course, we might use any combination of these:

1. experience (the five senses)
2. intuition (feeling)
3. reason
4. authority

At this point, I think it would be instructive if the reader would ponder these four categories considering which are the most or least helpful, whether or not they are related to each other, whether some should be used in combination, and whether the list is complete. The next few chapters will consider some of these issues.

For the present, we might take a brief look at intuition and authority which many would believe to be the weakest. Abraham Lincoln said that many times during the Civil War when it was difficult to know what to do, he would have a strong feeling that he should take a certain action and that whenever he acted on such a feeling, things turned out right, and when he did not, they went wrong. He believed that these feelings were guidance from God. Whether or not his intuition was truly divine or not is beyond the scope of this chapter. We will return to this issue later.

Even though many would believe that authority is not a good reason for knowledge, no less an expert on scientific knowledge than Karl Popper says that, "almost all our knowledge is traditional."[6] If you stop to think about that, I believe you will agree with it. Even in science most of what we "know" is the result of our teacher's or textbook's statements. Not even scientists have actually carried out more than a small number of experiments themselves. But we believe, on authority, that someone else has done the experiment and has accurately reported the results.

At this point it may seem that the difficulties in epistemology are so great that we should just forget about the whole thing and admit that we can never know anything. Some people, extreme skeptics, do just that. However, almost all people, even skeptics, act like they know some things. For example, they do not step out in front of a truck, if they "know" that a truck is traveling down the highway in front of them. For help with these difficulties, in the next chapter we will consider the point of view of mathematics, its strengths and weaknesses in and then in the following chapter do the same for science. With a little luck, or better, in the providence of God, we may eventually come to a better understanding.

Before going to the next chapter, I should tell you how I use the phrase "I know…" I think that three criteria must be met: I believe p, p is true, and I have adequate evidence for p. For any statement p, I have some degree of certainty in my mind. I could label that degree of certainty with a number between zero and one, with zero meaning I am certain it is false and one meaning I am certain it is true. In a sense, I agree with the skeptics that number is always between zero and one and perhaps never actually equal to one. However, when it gets sufficiently close to one, it sort of jumps to one and I say, "I know." What type and amount of evidence it takes for that to happen for me will be clearer to you, if you read the rest of this book. For some people, it will jump to one as soon as the number is greater than one-half; for others, it may need to be .999. In general, mathematicians require it to be extremely close to one. Probably, that is why most mathematicians' speech or writing usually contain many words such as probably, usually, and generally.

Mathematical Certainty

*"Mathematics is the study in which we never know what we are
talking about nor whether what we are saying is true."*

Bertrand Russell

"It is impossible to prove that there is a God," is a statement often
heard. Is it true or false? An understanding of the meaning of the
words is required before that question or any question can be properly
answered. In this case, the most crucial words are "prove," "God,"
"true" and "false." For the present, it is probably sufficient to say that
by the word "God," I mean what Christians have generally meant by
that word for the last two thousand years. By the word "true," I will
mean "is in agreement with reality," in keeping with the discussion in
chapter two. The word "false" just means the opposite of true.

What we need to concentrate on now is the meaning of the word
"prove." Abraham Lincoln, after he was a member of Congress, studied Euclidean geometry in order to find out what it meant to prove
something. As a lawyer, he had to prove various things to a judge or
jury and he wanted to know just what that meant. He felt, as most
people do, that mathematics is the place where certainty resides. Most
people who ask for a proof of the existence of God would probably say
that they mean a mathematical demonstration of God's existence. And
on further questioning, they would state that mathematical proof produces absolute certainty. Statements like "It's as certain as two and
two are four," or "It's a mathematical impossibility," indicate a belief
that in mathematics we have complete certainty. So, they are search-
ing for a logical argument that will convince every sane person that
there is a God.

What we need to examine is the nature of mathematical proof, its
relation to the "scientific method" and then the relation of each to other
areas including religious faith. It is my hope and belief that this will
shed some light on the relation between faith and reason. Mathematicians have not always meant the same thing by proof, so we must use a

historical approach.

Thales, who lived around 600 B.C. in Greece., is usually considered the father of mathematics because of his emphasis on proof. Before this time many peoples had worked with numbers and geometric shapes, the Egyptians, Babylonians, Chinese, Indians, and others, but none had used the deductive or mathematical method of proof. As a result, all cultures before the Greeks combined brilliant insights into mathematical relationships with incorrect formulas and rules. Einstein said,

> We reverence ancient Greece as the cradle of western science. Here for the first time the world witnessed the miracle of a logical system which proceeded from step to step with such precision that every single one of its propositions was absolutely indubitable—I refer to Euclid's geometry. This admirable triumph of reasoning gave the human intellect the necessary confidence in itself for its subsequent achievements.[1]

This is high praise from perhaps the greatest theoretical physicist of all time. Mathematicians appreciate this praise and appreciate the great achievements of the Greek mathematicians while giving a more cautious evaluation of Greek mathematics.

The mathematical method begun by Thales culminated 250 years later in *The Elements*, a masterful and logical arrangement of geometry by Euclid. The deductive method as used by the Greeks consisted of proving theorems by using the logical rules of Aristotle and starting from statements called axioms and postulates. An axiom was a general statement that was considered to be a self-evident truth. For example, one of Euclid's axioms was "The whole is greater than the part." A postulate was a geometrical statement so simple and obvious that its truth could be assumed. For example, "It is possible to draw a straight line from any point to any point," was Euclid's first postulate.

Axioms and postulates, in contrast to theorems, were never proved. There were two reasons for this. One, they were thought to be so obvious that they needed no proof. And two, it is impossible to prove every statement. In order to prove a statement, other statements must be used as reasons; to prove those reasons would require more, and so on and on. Therefore, since circular reasoning is not allowed in mathematics, one must start with some statements that are not proved. These were the axioms and postulates which the Greeks believed were obviously true. The deductive method as used by Euclid led to the proof of 465 theorems in *The Elements*. This method was so successful that one would expect it to be used in many other areas. Archimedes, one of the greatest mathematicians of all time, did use it in physics. His book *On Plane Equilibriums* contains proofs of 25 theorems on mechanics based on three postulates. Also, *On Floating Bodies* proves ten theorems of hydrostatics from only two postulates. But then, probably because of the decline of Greek culture, the method was not used in any systematic way for centuries, not even in algebra or other branches of mathematics.

Not until the Renaissance did the mathematical method begin to regain its popularity. In 1637 in *A Discourse on Method*, Descartes proposed that it could be used in all areas. He said,

> The long chains of perfectly simple and easy reasons, which geometers are accustomed to employ in order to arrive at their most difficult demonstrations, had given me reason to believe that all things which can fall under the knowledge of man succeed each other in the same way and that provided only we abstain from receiving as true any opinions which are not true, and always observe the necessary order in deducing one from the other, there can be none so remote that they may not be reached, or so hidden that they may not be discovered.[2]

All that was needed was to find the basic truths and then use logic.

Descartes, Spinoza, and many others attempted to apply this mathematical or deductive method in theology. "Starting from...premises, Hobbes and Locke each attempted to 'deduce' universal rules of political behavior and morals."[3] There was disagreement about how we know that the axioms are true. Descartes believed that some ideas are implanted in our minds by God. For Socrates and Plato, knowledge is inborn, while for Locke all axioms came from experience. Whether from intuition, experience, or revelation, all believed that there were self-evident truths and that the deductive method was a useful device to build on these truths. Therefore, many continued to try this deductive method in other areas of knowledge.

For example, in 1764, Beccaria, writing on some questions of law, stated, "These problems deserve to be solved with such geometrical precision as shall suffice to prevail over the clouds of sophistication, over seductive eloquence, or timid doubt."[4] A few years later, Helvetius, in claiming that men are reasonable, said, "That if words were precisely defined, and their definitions ranged in a dictionary, all the propositions of morality, politics, and metaphysics would become as susceptible of demonstration as the truths of geometry."[5]

Probably the best known of these attempts to use the deductive method outside of mathematics is in the Declaration of Independence. Jefferson started with these axioms, "We hold these truths to be self-evident, that all men are created equal, that they are endowed by their creator with certain unalienable rights, that among these are life, liberty, and the pursuit of happiness." He proceeded to establish one theorem: "These colonies are and of right ought to be free and independent states." During the debates over slavery just before the Civil War, Lincoln wrote, "One would start with great confidence that he could convince any sane child that the simple propositions of Euclid are true, but would fail utterly, with one who should deny the definitions and axioms. The principles of Jefferson are the definitions and axioms of free society."[6] Lincoln understood the deductive method and Jefferson's use of it in the establishment of our government although Lincoln obviously never tried to teach geometry to children!

These valiant attempts to use the deductive method met with mixed success. Even if Descartes was right that it is theoretically possible to use this method in all areas, it might be so difficult to carry out that it would be humanly impossible, or perhaps it would just take longer than was originally thought. But mathematicians were about to run into problems which changed their view of the deductive method. Before looking into this development, it might be well to summarize the mathematical method as understood at that time. (See Figure 4-1.)

Axioms   (self-evident truths)

⇓   (logic or deductive reasoning)

Theorems

Figure 4-1.

What changed mathematicians' minds about the deductive method was a development related to Euclid's fifth postulate. That postulate had always bothered mathematicians, even Euclid himself. Considering plane geometry only, that is, not three dimensional space, a modern equivalent of the fifth postulate is, "Through any given point, P, not on a given line, l, there is exactly one line, m, parallel to the given line." (See Figure 4-2.) That is, in a given plane, there is one and only one line passing through P which will never intersect l. From the very beginning, this postulate seemed more complicated than the other postulates. So many felt that it should be proved as a theorem instead of assumed as a postulate. Most of the great mathematicians of that period tried to prove it from the other postulates. It wasn't until the early nineteenth century that three mathematicians, Gauss, Bolyai, and Lobachevsky, independently discovered that it was impossible to prove postulate five using just the other postulates. In fact, it is possible to show that if the fifth postulate is replaced by one of its negations, (there exists more than one line through P parallel to l), the set of postulates is still consistent provided the original set of postulates for Euclidean geometry is consistent.

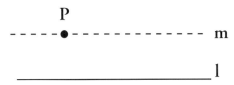

Figure 4-2.

That last sentence may seem a bit confusing to those not familiar with mathematics. Let me try to explain it. When we say that a set of postulates is consistent, we mean that they do not contradict each other, and no theorems that can be proved from them will contradict each other. In other words, no matter how many theorems will ever be proved from the postulates, it will never happen that one of the theorems will be a negation of another theorem or postulate. This is obviously a very difficult thing to prove. Until this development, with Euclid's fifth postulate, no one ever considered the possibility of geometry being not consistent. Since it was believed to be obviously true, it had to be consistent. But now, mathematicians had proved that the fifth postulate could be replaced by its negation, and that the system was as consistent as it was before. It is beyond the scope of our discussion to demonstrate this. There are readily available textbooks for any student of mathematics wishing to pursue it further.[7]

Of course, a set of statements could be consistent without being true. It is conceivable that a liar might still be consistent. But this, at least, raised the question, might the new set of postulates be the true set? But then the old Euclidean geometry would have to be false. It didn't seem at all likely, but it at least it suggested that it was a possibility. And beyond this, if, incredibly, Euclidean geometry turned out to be false, then we would not even know if either set of postulates was consistent.

Mathematicians began to play with the new set of postulates and called it a non-Euclidean geometry. Various non-Euclidean geometries could be obtained simply by taking one or more postulates and changing them in some way. At first this seemed to be no more than a strange but harmless game that mathematicians were playing. Philosophers and most people, including mathematicians, still believed that Euclidean geometry was true. Some non-Euclidean geometries were developed extensively. So now mathematicians were working with postulate sets which were not obviously true. I am not saying that were not true, just that it was not obvious that they were true. The postulates were just assumptions.

In these cases, at least, the mathematical method was no longer establishing theorems as indubitably true because they followed from self-evident truths; rather it was simply demonstrating that if the postulates were true, then the theorems would have to be true. One might argue that for about fifty years "real" mathematics was still establishing truths while a kind of "make-believe" mathematics was playing games. Then Albert Einstein used a non-Euclidean geometry as a basis for his theory of relativity, and physicists began acting as if non-Euclidean geometry were true, and as if the theory of relativity was not just an abstract physical theory with no relation to the real world. One of its practical consequences is the atomic bomb. Please note that practical does not necessarily mean good.

It became clear, then, that certainty was gone from mathematics, and no philosophy of mathematics is likely to restore it. Which of the geometries, if any, is true is not likely to be known. Kline, a twentieth century mathematician, says that mathematics "is a human construction and any attempt to find an absolute basis for it is probably doomed to failure."[8] But as Christians believing that God created our minds as well as everything else, don't we have an absolute basis? It seems not, at least in this life. As Gauss, one of the greatest mathematicians of all time, said,

> I am becoming more and more convinced that the physical necessity of our Euclidean geometry cannot be proved, at least not by human reason nor for human reason. Perhaps in another life we will be able to obtain insight into the nature of space which is now unattainable.[9]

The idea of alternative sets of axioms was not just an isolated event in geometry. When mathematicians discovered that they could create new geometries by tinkering with the postulate set, they began creating new algebras in the same way. Just as non-Euclidean geometries arose out of Euclidean geometry by altering the parallel postulate, Sir William Rowen Hamilton, an Irish mathematician, altered the axiom of commutativity and developed a new algebra. Soon many algebras developed out of the ordinary algebra of real numbers. And sure enough, a physicist, Werner Heisenberg, used one as a basis for quantum mechanics and hence for understanding the internal structure of atoms.

As a result of all this, mathematicians have come to regard axioms and postulates alike as synonyms for assumptions. Axioms are no longer considered by mathematicians as self-evident truths. They are assumptions, pure and simple. Mathematics consists of formally labeling certain statements "true" and then using logic to label other statements "true," or as stated earlier, demonstrating that if the axioms are true then the theorems are also true. The object is to establish relative truth, not absolute truth. This does not mean that mathematicians necessarily believe that there are no absolute truths, it just means that within the mathematical system it doesn't matter.

We can now decide whether there is a mathematical proof for the existence of God. There is. I often give a deductive proof for that in my mathematics classes. One just needs to start with the right assumptions. Obviously, anyone may object to the assumptions. Furthermore, if one starts with different assumptions, one could prove that God does not exist. It all depends on the axioms or assumptions. The person who demands a mathematical proof for God's existence does not understand what is meant by a mathematical proof. What he really wants is a logical argument that would convince any sane person.

So far it may seem as though my thesis is that mathematics is of no value. This is not the case. I have a great appreciation for the value of mathematics and the value of deductive or mathematical reasoning in all aspects of life, including religion. But it is necessary to understand the limitations of a method in order to really understand its value. And we must look at two more problems before emphasizing the positive side.

Remember that it is impossible to prove every statement because statements are needed as reasons which in turn would require reasons. Mathematics has been praised for its precision in language as well as its certainty. So one would expect all words in a mathematical system to be carefully defined. Euclid thought so and tried hard to do it. As a result he came up with some strange "definitions": "A point is that which has no part," and "A line is breadthless length"[10] When we try to define every word we are in a situation similar to that of trying to prove every statement. In order to define a word, one must use other words which, in turn, require further words for their definition and so on and on. Unless circular definitions are allowed (as in an ordinary dictionary), one must begin with a set of undefined words. These undefined terms are kept as simple as possible and the axioms or postulates give some of their properties. For example, "line" is usually one of the undefined terms but the postulates describe all of its properties that are required in the mathematical system. Some of its postulated properties include the following: "For every two points there is a line joining them" and "A line may be extended any required distance."

So, in mathematics we prove statements (called theorems) by starting with axioms and using logic or deductive reasoning. Then we are certain that our theorems are true, if our assumptions are true. But if our assumptions are in doubt, then we cannot be certain about our conclusions. And, we cannot use deductive reasoning to prove that our axioms are true, because as we have seen, every mathematical system must start with some assumptions. Therefore, in mathematics we can never arrive at certainty. But, at least, we would like to have consistency.

This change in mathematics from truth to consistency is illustrated by the statements of Thomas Jefferson and Abraham Lincoln. In the Declaration of Independence, Jefferson starts with "self-evident" truths to demonstrate our right to establish our own government. In the Gettysburg Address, Lincoln said,

> Four score and seven years ago our fathers brought forth upon this continent, a new nation, conceived in liberty and dedicated to the proposition that "all men are created equal.' Now we are engaged in a great Civil War testing whether that nation or any nation so conceived and so dedicated can long endure.

Notice the change in emphasis from Jefferson's words about "self-evident" truths. Lincoln was still dedicated to a government built on equality, but in 1863 it was not self-evident that such a government could endure. They were testing the consistency of the axioms with real life in nineteenth century America.

And then even consistency turned out to be a problem. Kurt Gödel, a mathematical logician, demonstrated in 1931 that if you have a set of axioms that is complete enough to give such a simple thing as the real number system, then it cannot be proved to be consistent. Notice that he did a very interesting thing. Only mathematicians do these kinds of things. He proved that it is impossible to prove that a particular set of axioms is consistent. He did not prove that the set of axioms is inconsistent, only that it is impossible to prove that it is a consistent set. Therefore, the system of real numbers, the usual numbers studied in high school mathematics, will never be proved to be consistent.

Now, of course, we believe that they are consistent, but that is exactly the point I am trying to make. We are reduced to the place where we must have faith. We cannot prove it. In fact, we even prove that we can't prove it. The history of mathematics has evolved from truth to consistency to faith. As one philosopher of mathematics has said,

> Suppose we loosely define a religion as any discipline whose foundations rest on an element of faith . . . . There may or may not be reason present, but at least there has to be some element of faith. Quantum mechanics, for example, would be a religion under this definition. But mathematics would hold the unique position of being the only branch of theology possessing a rigorous demonstration of the fact that it should be so classified.[11]

Because of this lack of certainty, it would seem as though we were in quite a quandary. However, we must remember that as Christians, we also believe that man is finite and fallen. Therefore, it does not seem unreasonable to me that our knowledge is imperfect. Our most important mathematical systems may never be known to be consistent, even without worrying about truth. Yet, what other creation of man has the beauty of mathematics as well as its manifold applications to our understanding of reality?

Though we are finite and fallen, we do not just give up. We try to get the best intuitive foundation we can, and we check our logical deductions against whatever kind of reality we can. The strength of mathematics comes from its many strands: reason, of course, but also intuition, experience, and tradition. The Christian answer to the problems in the foundations of mathematics is humility. This should be no great surprise since it is also the Christian answer to many other problems.

Now to return to the question of proofs for the existence of God. We have seen that in the mathematical sense of the word "prove," we can prove that there is a God. We just have to start with the right assumptions. But these assumptions may be in doubt, in which case the "proof" doesn't mean anything. On the other hand, if we mean by the word "prove," give a logical argument that will convince any sane person, then we cannot that God exists, but we cannot prove that God doesn't exist either.

Mathematical proof, then, consists of going from axioms to theorems by way of deductive reasoning. Axioms are sometimes called postulates or assumptions, and when this method is used in science they may be called hypotheses, presuppositions, and sometimes even laws. Today, a set of assumptions used in science is often called a model. It is important to note that deductive reasoning cannot lead us to these axioms. Then what good is deductive reasoning? I believe there are at least two very important benefits that come from deductive reasoning.

I. If through observation, experience, revelation, or any other method we come to <u>believe</u> something (let's call them axioms), then reason can be used to deduce other things (let's call them conclusions). That is, if our axioms are true, then our conclusions are true also and we have become aware of new truths or at least truth in a new and perhaps more useful form. Thus, we may have as much confidence (or at least almost as much confidence) in our conclusions as we had in our original axioms.

II. The conclusions can be used to test the original axioms. If the conclusions agree with our experience, we have even more faith in our axioms. But if the conclusions do not agree with our experience, our faith in the axioms <u>may</u> be weakened or destroyed.

Now, let us consider how the mathematical method (i.e., deductive reasoning), the scientific method, and faith in divine revelation are related. At first thought, it would seem that revelation and the scientific method have nothing in common. However, when we consider the question, "Is a particular proposition or set of propositions a divine revelation?" it sounds a lot like the question, "Is a particular proposition or set of propositions a good scientific model or theory?" Perhaps there is some similarity in the way we might answer these questions. Before attempting an answer let us consider the scientific method in the next chapter.

Scientific Fact

"In error are those theorists who believe that theory comes inductively from experience."

Einstein

If certainty does not reside in mathematics, what about science? If something is "a scientific fact," is it not, therefore, unquestionably true? Scientific facts are established by "the scientific method," a method widely revered in Western society. But what is the scientific method?

There may not even be such a thing as the scientific method. There are certainly different methods or procedures in different sciences, for example; the very important method of repeated experiments is not possible in some parts of astronomy, biology, and geology. Even so, I believe there are some common elements to all scientific investigations. I intend to identify some of them and will label that "the scientific method." It will not completely define the scientific endeavor or even any one branch of science, however, what I will call the scientific method is something significant which is common to all of science. I trust it will be helpful in our study of science and later religion.

As a starting point, we will look at a popular, though over-simplified description of the scientific method. A scientist gathers and organizes data. He then uses inductive reasoning to make generalizations, which he might call theories but for ease of discussion and comparison with the mathematical method, I will call postulates. At this point in the method the scientist would agree that he is postulating these laws on the basis of his data. He will check the postulates against all the data he possesses and may devise new experiments to further test the generalizations.

Deductive reasoning is involved in the testing. The postulates imply that under specific conditions certain precise results must occur. If the scientist can contrive these specific conditions and observe the predicted results, his confidence in the postulates increases. Furthermore, these postulates may be used as premises and by means of deductive reasoning additional generalizations (we will call these theorems) can be derived. These, of course, can be tested in the same way as the postulates. At each testing time new data is obtained which may cause the scientist to modify the postulates and the cycle of steps repeated. It is the scientists belief that, in the long run, this procedure gives closer and closer approximations to the truth about reality. Figure 5-1 illustrates this procedure.

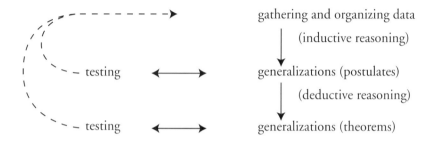

Figure 5-1.

Before looking at an example of this process, we should consider a problem at the very top of the diagram. How does one gather data? Are there little hunks of data lying around just waiting to be picked up and organized into a theory? As Tolstoy has said,

> Contemporary science investigates facts. But what facts? Why those particular facts and not others? Scientists of today are very fond of saying solemnly and confidently: 'We only investigate facts' imagining these words to have meaning. One cannot possibly only investigate facts for the number of facts is <u>innumerable</u>…Before investigating the facts one must have a theory on the basis of which such or such facts are selected from the innumerable quantity. And such a theory exists and is even very definitely expressed, though many of those engaged in contemporary science either ignore it, that is, do not wish to know it, or actually do not know it, or pretend not to.[1]

Good scientists who have thought about the methods of science agree with Tolstoy. The astronomer Tycho Brahe asserted that "it was impossible to sit down just to observe without the guidance of any hypothesis at all."[2]   So here's the problem: facts lead to theories, but theories must come before facts. Which came first, theories or facts? Like the chicken and the egg, each must come before the other.

In a painting by M.C. Escher, there are two hands: a left hand drawing the right one at the same time that the right one is drawing the left. A paradox but not a contradiction since transcending the two dimensional canvas, there was a three dimensional hand (Escher's) which drew them both. I do not know how, but I believe that God created our minds so in tune with the rest of His creation that the whole scientific process works even though it seems that we must have facts before we can devise theories but still need theories before we can have facts.

As an example of the scientific method, the ancient Greek astronomers observed the sun, moon, and stars. From this data, by induction, came an easy generalization or postulate: all heavenly bodies travel around the earth in circular paths. As they checked this postulate, they found that it gave accurate results for all heavenly bodies except a very few stars that they called wandering stars or planets. These exceptions, however, forced a modification of the postulate. They then decided that all heavenly bodies travel around the earth in circular paths, or else they travel in circular paths around a point that in turn is traveling around the earth in a circular path. This is essentially the Ptolemaic theory, a geocentric model of astronomy. (See Figure 5-2.)

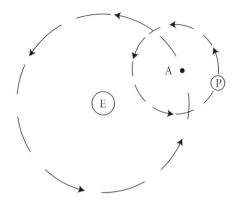

Figure 5.2.
E represents the earth, P represents a planet traveling in a circle about A, while A itself is revolving about the earth.

At this point, I hope that the reader is saying to himself that although it seems reasonable that the first postulate came by induction, the second seems to come out of thin air. I hope that is the reader's reaction, because it is certainly mine. Something more than induction alone was at work there, something we might call creative genius. This is a point we must return to later. Now, however, it will help us to understand how the Greeks arrived at this modified postulate if we look at some of their other assumptions. They believed that the earth was imperfect, the heavens perfect, and that circular motion was the only perfect motion. Knowing these assumptions, we can more easily see how they arrived at each of the postulates, even though creativity was still involved in arriving at the modified postulate. This also illustrates the fact that there are always presuppositions in a scientist's mind at the top of Figure 5-1, and that these presuppositions determine what the scientist calls a fact. To the Greeks, it was a scientific fact that the stars traveled around the earth. It would have seemed preposterous to them if anyone would have suggested that this "fact" was determined by their presuppositions and that furthermore, they were forcing the data to fit their assumptions.

From their postulates about the paths of the sun, moon, and planets the Greeks could accurately predict when eclipses would occur and when conjunctions of the various planets would happen. Remember that when conclusions agree with reality, one's faith in the premises usually increases. Thus, fulfilled predictions based on these geocentric hypotheses increased people's faith in the Ptolemaic theory. Notice that although it increased people's faith in the Ptolemaic theory, fulfilled predictions could never prove the theory. There are always other hypotheses that will agree with the data. Copernicus and Kepler later elaborated a heliocentric theory that accounted for the same facts and in a simpler manner but for nearly two thousand years the Ptolemaic theory was believed because its predictions were verified. That is, it worked.

When Copernicus suggested that the earth traveled around the sun instead of vice versa, theologians were upset because they thought that he was contradicting the Bible. But it was also argued that the heliocentric theory did not agree with the facts. If the earth traveled around the sun then the star field should appear different in March than it would six months later in September because the earth would then be on the opposite side of the sun. See Figure 5-3 for a special example in which the bright star A and the dimmer star B would appear to change sides. This phenomenon is called parallax and the reader can experience it on a smaller scale simply by alternately viewing the world by closing one eye and then the other.

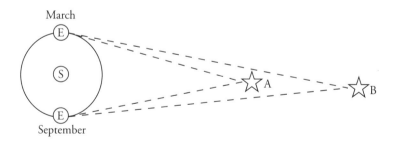

Figure 5-3.

Copernicus' antagonists said that the star field should appear different when viewed six months apart but, in fact, no such difference could be observed by them at that time. Therefore, they claimed that Copernicus must be wrong. His theory disagreed with the 'facts.' People like Copernicus and Kepler liked the theory so well because it was so much simpler than the Ptolemaic that they refused to give up on it just because of a few "facts." In fact, Morris Kline, a mathematician and mathematical historian, claims that they believed that their theories were true because they were beautiful.[3] Today, of course, scientists believe in the heliocentric theory and explain the apparent discrepancy by a belief that the stars are so much farther away from us than had been supposed then and that is why parallax could not be observed by the unaided eye. This is another example of the "facts" (no parallax) being determined by theory (belief concerning the size of the universe). With modern precision tools parallax has been observed. Does this mean that we now have absolute knowledge that the geocentric theory is false and heliocentric theory true? Of course not! We do have a lot more evidence that supports the heliocentric theory, but it is just one astronomical model (the best one at present). It is always possible that some day a better model will be found. In fact, the history of science shows that one model is generally superseded by another.

As another example of the scientific method as shown in Figure 5-1, consider Isaac Newton who observed various falling bodies (including apples and the moon). From this data he hypothesized that there is a force of attraction between every two objects that is directly proportional to the product of their masses and inversely proportional to the square of the distance between them, expressed mathematically, $F = \dfrac{k\, m_1 m_2}{d^2}$. From this formula he could deduce Kepler's Laws of planetary motion and many other things. Newton himself believed that this was the way the scientific method operated. In spite of Newton's belief, there seems to me to be a serious flaw in the whole scheme and that is the step where he claimed that he went from the data to the formula by induction alone. It is certainly clear that Newton did go from the data to the formula, but I think that there must be more involved than inductive reasoning. One view is that it is not induction at all.

In 1934 Karl Popper revolutionized philosophy of science when he said that justifying inductive reasoning is neither possible nor necessary. Popper said scientific theories aren't derived inductively from facts. They're invented as hypotheses, speculations, guesses, then subjected to experimental test in which critics try to refute them. A theory is scientific, said Popper, if it's in principle capable of being tested, risking refutation. If a theory survives such testing, it gains credibility, and may be tentatively established; but it's never proved. Even if a scientific theory is objectively true, we can never know it to be so with certainty.[4]

Even so, I prefer to keep inductive reasoning as a part of the scientific method and add extra things to it.

Figure 5-4 is a modification of Figure 5-1 that shows some of these extra things. Please notice particularly the last of the added elements.

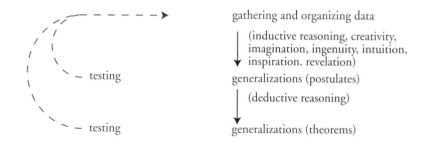

Figure 5-4.

Before we further examine these additions to the scientific method, remember that the scientist does not begin at the top of these diagrams with a completely open or unbiased mind. He has various presuppositions, attitudes, and inclinations determined by his culture, psychological make-up, and overall vision of the world. It is also possible, and even probable, that his participation in the scientific endeavor will modify these.

A recent example of some scientists' world view affecting the scientific endeavor is astronomers' difficulty with the Big Bang theory.

In 1965, Penzias and Wilson discovered a background radiation coming from every direction in the heavens. No theory has been found to account for this radiation except an initial explosion out of which all of the universe came. This is called the Big Bang theory and it implied a beginning, a creation and thus the possibility of a creator. At that time, most astronomers believed that the universe always existed, that there was no beginning. Because this disagreed with their presuppositions they resisted the theory. Einstein said that the Big Bang theory "irritates me."[5] Eddington wrote that it "is repugnant to me...is preposterous...it leaves me cold."[6] Phillip Morrison of MIT said "I would like to reject it."[7] The astronomer Robert Jastrow says,

> Their reactions provide an interesting demonstration of the response of the scientific mind—supposedly a very objective mind—when evidence uncovered by science itself leads to a conflict with articles of faith in our profession. It turns out that the scientist behaves the way the rest of us do when our beliefs are in conflict with the evidence. We become irritated, we pretend the conflict does not exist, or we paper it over with meaningless phrases.[8]

Eventually, though, astronomers have had to admit that the Big Bang theory is the best available at the present time.

One presupposition that a scientist must have is a firm faith that the universe is orderly and that this order is accessible to man's mind. Alfred North Whitehead expressed it thus: a scientist must have "the inexpugnable belief that every detailed occurrence can be correlated with its antecedent in a perfectly definite manner exemplifying general principles." This faith was necessary before science could develop. Until it did, most people did not have this belief, and Whitehead raised the question, "How has this conviction been so vividly planted on the European mind?" It certainly was not any kind of obvious induction from observation. His answer is, "It must come from the medieval insistence on the rationality of God, conceived as with the personal energy of Jehovah and with the rationality of a Greek philosopher."[9]

Imagination is one of the most important ingredients in the scientific method. Physicist Werner Heisenberg said, "In fact, imagination plays a decisive role in natural science. For even though we can hope to get at the facts only after many sober and careful experiments, we can fit the facts themselves together only if we can <u>feel</u> rather than think our way into the phenomena."[10]   Einstein would even say that Figure 5-4 is not just a modification of Figure 5-1 but a totally different process. In his view,

> The best path to be followed might not be that of observation followed by induction of general laws, but the totally different process of postulating a theory and then discovering whether or not the facts fitted it. Thus a theory should start with more scientific and philosophical assumptions than the facts alone warranted.[11]

One of these assumptions was his belief in the harmony of the universe.

I think that the role of imagination in science has been vastly underestimated by many, even by some scientists. At a recent conference of natural scientists, the speaker talked about imagination as a part of the scientific endeavor. In the discussion period following his presentation several scientists raised rather violent objections to the reference to the importance of imagination in science. In the discussion one of them used the pejorative phrase "figment of imagination" in place of the word "imagination." Observation, reason, objectivity have been rightly emphasized in science, but for some it seems that this emphasis has blinded them to the need for imagination also. We must remember that, as the biochemist Denis Alexander has said, "There is no such thing as 'pure objectivity.' Rather there is a continuum between the objective and the subjective."[12]

All of the great scientists who have considered the matter agree that imagination is essential. Einstein wrote, "The finest emotion of which we are capable is the mystic emotion. Herein lies the germ of all true science. Anyone to whom this feeling is alien, who is no longer capable of wonderment and lives in a state of fear is a dead man."[13] Einstein's colleague and friend Philipp Franck said,

For Einstein the fundamental theoretical laws are a free creation of the imagination, the product of the activity of an inventor whose speculations are limited by two principles: one empirical according to which the conclusion drawn from the theory must be confirmed by experience, and a semilogical, semiaesthetic principle according to which the fundamental laws should be as few as possible and compatible with logic.[14]

Anyone who is interested in further exploring Einstein's thought on this matter should read his essay "On the Method of Theoretical Physics."[15]

The brilliant mathematician, logician, and philosopher Bertrand Russell discussed the relationships between mystical feeling, revelation, insight, reason and the scientific attitude in the following passages: "I yet believe that by sufficient restraint, there is an element of wisdom to be learned from the mystical way of feeling, which does not seem to be obtained in any other manner."[16] He explains what he means by the mystical way of feeling by saying that mystics have a "belief in the possibility of a way of knowing which may be called revelation or insight or intuition, as contrasted with sense, reason, and analysis."[17] Of course, Russell has a high regard for reason as a test for whatever is suggested by insight: "What I do wish to maintain—and it is here that the scientific attitude becomes imperative—is that insight, untested and unsupported, is an insufficient guarantee of truth, in spite of the fact that much of the most important truth is first suggested by its means."[18] He concludes, "In fact, the opposition of instinct and reason is mainly illusory. Instinct, intuition, or insight is what first leads us to the beliefs."[19] In other words, the creative impulse comes from intuition, imagination, and revelation, but reason must be used to evaluate, test, make judgments, guide, and, in fact, govern.

Therefore, perhaps a better way of looking at the scientific method would be to call the set of postulates a theory or model. This model is obtained in some way from data by means of induction, imagination, inspiration, etc. It seems to me not unlikely that at times God gives some revelation of a scientific nature to a scientist, whether the scientist is a Christian or not. Perhaps "illumination" would be a more appropriate word than "revelation." In any case, God works in mysterious ways his wonders to perform. In whatever way this model is obtained, it is essential that reason be used to determine whether or not it is an acceptable one. It must be checked against all kinds of evidence. It will probably seem to be in conflict with some of the evidence, which usually is a surprise to most non-scientists. Remember that the Copernican model was in conflict with the "facts." Therefore, the scientist does not discard a model just because it contains some paradoxes. He will compare it with other models. None will be able to explain everything. All will probably involve paradoxes. None can be proved by a single line of reasoning, so cumulative evidence will be important in determining in which of the various models the scientist will place his faith. From this time on, the behavior of the scientist will depend, at least in part, on which model he believes in and the degree of that belief.

Gospel Truth

Take all of this Book upon reason that you can,
and the balance on faith."

Abraham Lincoln

How can one know that the Gospel is true? There have been many deductive proofs of the existence of God. Anyone who is convinced by one of these proofs still may be a long way from a belief in Christianity. But perhaps the real trouble with these proofs is the basic problem of any deductive proof which is that they must begin with assumptions. Each philosopher who has given a proof that there is a God believed that his assumptions were true, in fact, self-evident. But, as we have seen even in mathematics, there is no agreement about what is self-evident truth. Before the Fall, there were probably self-evident truths. But then no proof of God's existence was needed because the existence and even the nature of God were self-evident.

One answer to the question raised at the beginning of this chapter is that the truth of the Gospel has been divinely revealed to us. But how do we recognize a divine revelation? Suppose you receive what you think is a divine revelation. How do you know, in fact, that it is a revelation and not just the result of an idea planted in your subconscious mind from the combination of a television show you saw last week and a dream you had last night, perhaps aided by a touch of indigestion or the sight of a beautiful sunset? I think we would have to use the same kind of testing we use for a scientific theory. John Locke put it this way,

> Whatever God has revealed is certainly true: no doubt can be made of it. This is the proper object of faith: but whether it be a divine revelation or not, reason must judge... God when He makes the prophet does not unmake the man... I do not mean that we must consult reason and examine whether a proposition revealed from God can be made out by natural principles and if it cannot then we must reject it: but consult it we must.[1]

Notice that revelation, not reason, is the source of knowledge, but reason is an evaluator, a governor. Even in science we have seen that the great scientists admit that feeling, intuition, or even revelation may be the source of the theory, but reason must evaluate. In science it does not matter at all where or how the theory or model originates; what is important is that reason test it.

Therefore, the Gospel, that is, the Biblical or Christian view of reality, cannot be obtained as a logical conclusion from a set of assumptions that every person would accept, but it can be evaluated in somewhat the same way any other model of reality can be tested. We cannot use reason to arrive at this Biblical view of reality, but we can use reason to check it out. Note also that we can say the very same thing about Einstein's theory of relativity. We may not be able to use reason to arrive at it, but we can and must check it by the use of reason.

At this point, I would like to look at what the Bible says about reason, not to convince unbelievers that Christianity is true, although some of it may be helpful for that purpose, but rather to convince Christians that the methods of mathematics and science, namely reason and experience, are legitimate tools in the defense of Christianity. Peter tells us, "Always be prepared to make a defense to anyone who calls you to account for the hope that is in you, yet do it with gentleness and reverence." (I Peter 3:15) We may use reason, but love must accompany it.

God expects us to use reason and to look at the evidence. "Come let us reason together, says the Lord" (Isaiah 1:18). "I will instruct you and teach you in the way you should go: I will counsel you with my eye upon you. Be not like a horse or mule, without understanding, which must be curbed with a bit and bridle" (Psalm 32:8-9). So God will teach us, but He expects us to have more reasoning ability than a mule. Acts 9:22 tells us that Paul "confounded the Jews who lived in Damascus by proving that Jesus was the Christ." Acts 17:2 and 3 explain that this proof rested on the assumption that the scriptures were true, an assumption agreed to by the Jews.

In Athens, Paul had to change his starting point to reach common ground with the Greeks. In his sermon on Mars Hill, he does not appeal to the Jewish scriptures since the Greeks would not accept them as axiomatic. Instead, he appeals to elements in their religion and poetry and to recent events, the crucifixion and resurrection of Jesus Christ. Some have said that this approach was ineffective and that Paul should have stuck with his usual approach. As evidence for this they note that we hear nothing about a church being established at Athens, and there is no letter from Paul to the Athenians. However, we do know that more than two Athenians became believers, including at least one member of the Areopogus. We also know that the Bereans were more noble than the Thessalonians, but we have no Epistle to the Bereans. Besides, it is hard to see how the Old Testament would have convinced the Greeks of anything. Some common ground had to be found.

In the Old Testament, Samuel appeals to both history and miracles in I Samuel 12:6-18 to convince the Israelites to fear the Lord. Prophets throughout the Old Testament appealed to history to show the character as well as the existence of God. In the New Testament, also, this is true. Hebrews 11 recites many incidents from Old Testament history and Hebrews 12:1 begins, "Therefore, since we are surrounded by so great a cloud of witnesses. . . ." These men and women of faith referred to in the eleventh chapter are witnesses to the existence and nature of God.

Isaiah 4:20-29 tells us that fulfilled prophecy is evidence. Pascal points out the importance of fulfilled prophecy and furthermore that these prophecies came to us from a people who are noted for their zeal in preserving the accuracy of their documents and who did not understand the prophecies and so could not be accused of manipulating them to mean what they wanted them to mean. As Pascal says, "They, the people least open to suspicion in the world of favoring us, the most strict and zealous that can be named for their law and their prophets, have kept the books incorrupt."[2] There are many New Testament examples of the use of reason. The blind man who was healed by Jesus claimed, "Never since the world began has it been heard that anyone opened the eyes of a man born blind. If this man were not from God, he could do nothing." (John 9:32-33). The logical conclusion is that this man, Jesus, is from God. Peter asserts, "we did not follow cleverly devised myths when we made known to you the power and coming of our Lord Jesus Christ, but we were eyewitnesses of his majesty." (II Peter 1:16). John also claims to be an eyewitness in John 21:24 and very eloquently and movingly in I John 1:1-4. In his gospel he asserts, "Now Jesus did many other signs in the presence of the disciples, which are not written in this book; but these are written that you may believe that Jesus is the Christ, the Son of God, and that believing you may have life in His name" (John 20:30, 31).

Nature itself is a witness. "The heavens are telling the glory of God and the firmament proclaims his handiwork. Day to day pours forth speech, and night to night declares knowledge. There is no speech, nor are there words; their voice is not heard; yet their voice goes out through all the earth, and their words to the end of the world" (Psalm 19:1-4). Likewise, Paul says, "What can be known about God is plain to them, because God has shown it to them, namely, his eternal power and deity, has been clearly perceived in the things that have been made" (Rom. 1:19,20).

Romans 2 seems to suggest that something like self-evident truth "is written on their hearts," but also that there is confusion in their thoughts due to their fallen nature. "When Gentiles who have not the law do by nature what the law requires, they are a law to themselves, even though they do not have the law. They show that what the law requires is written on their hearts, while their conscience also bears witness and their conflicting thoughts accuse or perhaps excuse them on that day when, according to my gospel, God judges the secrets of men by Christ Jesus" (Rom. 2:14-16).

Jesus sometimes refused to give a sign of his divinity but never refused to help those who were sincerely seeking and who would be convinced by more evidence. When Thomas was told by the other disciples that Jesus was alive again, he said, "Unless I see in his hands the print of the nails, and place my hand in his side, I will not believe." This was a pretty strong statement! But eight days later, Jesus suddenly appeared within a closed room where the disciples were and said to Thomas, "Put your finger here, and see my hands; and put out your hand, and place it in my side; do not be faithless, but believing" (John 20:27). Thomas' answer was, "My Lord and my God."

Another example of looking at the evidence and Jesus' willingness to supply more is the experience of John the Baptist. After baptizing Jesus, John saw "the Spirit of God descending like a dove and alighting on him; and lo, a voice from heaven, saying, 'This is my beloved Son, with whom I am well pleased'" (Matt. 3:16-17). Later, John explains how he was sure that Jesus was the Son of God. God had told him that the person upon whom he would see the Spirit of God descend and remain would be the Messiah; thus when this revelation was fulfilled John knew that God had spoken to him, he knew who Jesus was, and he knew the importance of believing in Jesus (John 1:29-34 and John 3:22-26). So John believed because of the evidence, but later when he was in prison, his emotions got the better of him and he began to doubt. Then he sent his disciples to ask Jesus, "Are you he who is to come, or shall we look for another?" (Matt. 11:3). It would seem that if ever Jesus would be impatient with unbelief it would be now since John the Baptist had seen the sign that he had been told would signify the Messiah, but instead Jesus tells them to look at the evidence. "Go and tell John what you hear and see: the blind receive their sight and the lame walk, lepers are cleansed and the deaf hear, and the dead are raised up, and the poor have good news preached to them" (Matt. 11:4-5). John would understand that these signs were the fulfillment of Isaiah's prophecy. (Isaiah 35:4-6 and Isaiah 42:6-8). Jesus was not upset with John's doubt because he knew John's human weakness and also his sincere desire to know. In fact, instead of being upset, Jesus said, "Truly, I say to you, among those born of women there has arisen no one greater than John the Baptist" (Matt. 11:11).

Therefore, I believe the Bible expects us to use reason to evaluate the truth of Christianity. It is possible to look at Christianity as a theory in much the same way that we look at any theory in science. Does Christianity as a model for reality agree with our experience better than any other model? In order to sharpen the focus, consider the fact that millions of people have believed that Jesus is Lord, the Son of God, true God, of one substance with the Father. In short, millions believe that Jesus of Nazareth is God. Following is a list of all of the possible hypotheses that I can think of to account for this widespread belief. All hypotheses after H_0 assume that Jesus is not God.

H_0: Jesus is God

H_1: Christians have incorrectly interpreted parts of the New Testament as claims that Jesus is God.

H_2: The New Testament was written centuries after the events it relates and so is unreliable.

H_3: Basically, the New Testament was written in the first century, but the passages claiming the divinity of Jesus were added later.

H_4: The New Testament writers claimed that Jesus was God but knew that he was not God.

H_5: The new Testament writers believed that Jesus was God because they misunderstood Jesus.

H_6: Jesus claimed to be God when he knew that he was not God. (Liar Hypothesis)

H_7: Jesus believed that he was God, but he was mistaken. (Lunatic Hypothesis)

Readers of Josh McDowell or C. S. Lewis will recognize this list as an elaboration of their "Liar, Lunatic or Lord" argument. However, I believe that the added detail here is important for someone who is really seeking to know whether or not Christianity is true. Following is a brief discussion of these hypotheses. It is certainly not meant to be complete, but may be helpful as an outline for anyone who wishes to study it more completely. My belief is that hypotheses one through seven can reasonably be rejected, leaving us with H_0.

Sometimes Christians reject H_1 by pointing out the many passages which call Jesus the Son of God, the Christ, or the Messiah. We Christians have long believed that these terms mean that Jesus is God. I believe that He is, but not on the basis of those words. Even the god in the movie "Oh, God" said that Jesus really was his son . . . and so were Gandhi, Buddha, and every other person. So, many people believe that Jesus is God's son, but not in any unique way. The Christ, or the Messiah were terms used to refer to someone special whom the Jews believed would come to their aid sometime. Now the Jews certainly did not believe that the Messiah would be equal to God. Thus the claims that Jesus was the Son of God, the Christ, or the Messiah do not necessarily refute H_1.

One of the strongest statements of the divinity of Jesus is found in the first chapter of John. "In the beginning was the Word, and the Word was with God, and <u>the Word was God</u>. He was in the beginning with God, all things are made by God through him and without him was not anything made that was made. In him was life and that life was the light of men" (John 1:1-3). This passage certainly makes the claim that the Word was God and a later section of the same chapter equates the Word with Jesus.

> And the Word became flesh and dwelt among us, full of grace and truth; we have beheld his glory, glory as of the only Son from the Father (John bore witness to him, and cried, 'This was he of whom I said, "He who comes after me ranks before me, for he was before me."') and from his fullness have we all received grace upon grace. For the law was given through Moses; grace and truth came through Jesus Christ. No one has ever seen God; the only Son, who is in the bosom of the Father, he has made him known. (John 1:14-18)

Incidentally, I believe that this shows that the title "Son of God" is used in the New Testament in a unique sense.

Jesus is said to be the creator in several places. (Eph. 3: 9, Col.1:16-17, Heb. 1:2). There are also some indirect, but very strong, evidence that Jesus claimed to be God. In John 10:30, Jesus says, "I and the

Father are one." The Jews who heard that statement attempted to the stone him because of blasphemy, as they said, "because you, being a man, make yourself God" (John 10:33). So the people who were there understood it is as a claim that He was God. In Mark 14: 61-64, the high priest asked, "Are you the Christ, the Son of the Blessed?" and Jesus said "I am; and you will see the Son of Man sitting at the right hand of Power, and coming with the clouds of heaven." This seems to me to be more than just a claim of humanity. At least the council condemned him for blasphemy.

When a paralytic was brought to Jesus to be healed, Jesus said, "My son, your sins are forgiven." (Mark 2:1-13). Some of the scribes who were there were thinking, "This is blasphemy, only God can forgive sins." Jesus understood what they were thinking and said to them, "...To prove to you that the Son of Man has full authority to forgive sins on earth, I say to you (the paralytic) get up, pick up your bed and go home." I believe that this passage logically implies that Jesus was claiming to be God.

Men like Joseph, Daniel, and Paul always made it clear that they should not be worshiped, and when they were given credit for a miracle, they insisted that it was God who did it, not them. In contrast, Jesus accepted credit and worship. One incident is recorded in John 20:28 where Thomas says, "my Lord and my God." I believe these examples constitute enough evidence that the New Testament really does claim that Jesus is God. Keep in mind that all I am saying at this point is that the New Testament makes that claim. Whether or not the claim is true depends on the reliability of the New Testament and that is why we need to look at the remaining hypotheses.

Some have claimed that the New Testament was written long after the events it describes took place and therefore is unreliable. There is now good evidence that that is not the case. It was written within a few decades of the crucifixion, all before 100 A.D. and early manuscripts verify the accuracy of our present text. Three short but excellent books on this subject are *New Testament Documents: Are They Reliable?* by

F. F. Bruce, *History and Christianity* by John W. Montgomery, and *Can We Trust the New Testament?* by John A. T. Robinson. It is interesting that the last book, written by a liberal theologian, basically agrees with the conclusion of the two more conservative authors.

To decide about H_3, one needs to read the entire New Testament to see if it all fits together or if the claims of divinity could have been added later. I think that the evidence I have cited to refute H_1 shows that the claims of divinity permeate the New Testament and could not have just been added to the original documents. I would challenge anyone who doubts this to read the New Testament with this hypothesis in mind.

If H_1, H_2, and H_3 are rejected, then the claim that Jesus is God was made within thirty years of his death. H_4 and H_5 say that the disciples lied or misunderstood Jesus. If the Gospels are fiction, it is fiction of a type that was not written anywhere else for many centuries, according to C. S. Lewis, a literary critic and literary historian. It is hard to imagine that eleven men (not to mention 120) could agree to such a preposterous claim and all stick to it through persecution for the rest of their lives. The crucifixion and resurrection are crucial at this point. In the book *Who Moved the Stone?*, Frank Morison tells how he set out to show that the resurrection did not take place but in the process was convinced that it did. Now the disciples may have been deluded, but many saw the resurrected Lord, so it would have had to be mass delusion. Furthermore, as Paul said, these events were not done in a corner. The enemies of Christianity could not prove them wrong. Thousands and thousands were convinced by the disciples. As Bruce says, "the one interpretation which best accounts for all the data, as well as the abiding sequel, is that Jesus' bodily resurrection from the dead was a real and objective event."[3]

Part of the argument in the preceding paragraph applies to H_6 and H_7 also. To believe that Jesus was a great teacher but reject his main teaching seems strange, to say the least. Even though Albert Schweitzer did claim that Jesus was a great teacher but was deluded on the one point of his divinity, it seems incredible to me that someone as sane as Jesus appears to be in the Gospels could be so fantastically deluded as to believe he was God when he was not. Again, I would challenge anyone to read the New Testament in the light of H_6 or H_7 to see if those hypotheses make sense. In *Miracles*, C. S. Lewis states:

> The historical difficulty of giving for the life, sayings and influence of Jesus any explanation that is not harder than the Christian explanation, is very great. The discrepancy between the depth and sanity and (let me add) *shrewdness* of His moral teaching and the rampant megalomania which must lie behind His theological teaching unless He is indeed God, has never been satisfactorily got over.[4]

In *Mere Christianity*, C. S. Lewis states it even more colorfully:

> I am trying to prevent anyone saying the really foolish thing that people often say about Him: "I'm ready to accept Jesus as a great moral teacher, but I don't accept His claim to be God." That is the one thing we must not say. A man who said the sort of things Jesus said would not be a great moral teacher. He would be a lunatic – on a level with the man who says he is a poached egg – or else he would be the Devil of Hell. You must make your choice. Either this man was and is, the Son of God: or else a madman or something worse. You can shut Him up for a fool, you can spit at Him and kill Him for demon; or you can fall at his feet and call Him Lord and God.[5]

Therefore, I believe there are good reasons for rejecting hypotheses one through seven. That leaves us with H_0. Jesus is God. I must repeat that I realize I have not given conclusive arguments against these hypotheses. But I believe that the scheme should be helpful to anyone who is seriously seeking to know the truth. And I hope that I have given some evidence and some help in how to pursue the investigation in more depth.

The Bible gives us a particular view of reality. We are expected to think about it. God does not expect a blind leap of faith. A leap of faith, yes, but not a blind one. In all human affairs, a leap of faith is necessary since we never have complete knowledge before acting. So in that respect, Christianity is not different from any other area of life. If the leap of faith were completely blind, then we might equally well leap in any direction: to Christianity, Hinduism, Pantheism, or atheism. I believe that God wants us to look at the evidence and use reason. Following is a list, although certainly not a complete list, of some of the types of evidence for the Biblical or Christian view of reality.

1. The existence of moral law
2. The existence of personality
3. The truth of Biblical statements that can be verified
4. Historical evidence of Biblical events
5. Personal experience and the personal experience of other Christians
6. Scientific evidence
7. The weakness of alternative (i.e., non-Christian) models
8. Aesthetic reasons.

In *Mere Christianity* and *The Abolition of Man*, C. S. Lewis establishes the fact that almost all men acknowledge, by their actions if not by their words, the existence of a moral law. This is evidence that there is a God, a lawgiver, which is a step towards Christianity. Abraham Lincoln believed that the moral code found in the Bible was evidence that the Bible was divinely inspired. Lincoln said, "It seems to me that nothing short of infinite wisdom could by any possibility have devised and given to man this excellent and perfect moral code."[6]

Another evidence for a personal God is given by Elton Trueblood. He argues that since we experience personality, our own and others around us, and since personality could not arise from an impersonal universe, a personal God must have created us.

There are many Biblical statements that can be checked by our experience or by the results of natural or social science. *None of These Diseases* by Dr. S. I. McMillan, shows that many of God's commands to the Israelites make sense in the light of modern medical knowledge: knowledge that would not have been available to the Israelites of that time. Recently, a friend who was a humanist with a very optimistic view of man's nature, commented that it begins to appear that man is basically selfish. He seemed unaware that he was discovering what the Bible clearly says about man's fallen nature. To use J. B. Phillip's phrase, what the Bible says about the nature of man has the "ring of truth."

The fourth point in the list may not sound like part of the scientific method, but Heisenberg said, "Science, too, is based on personal experience, or on the experience of others reliably reported."[7] I think most people would be surprised by how much of what a scientist believes does not come directly from his own experience but from his faith in the reports of other scientist's experience. Of course, there is much checking of one scientist's experience with the experience of other scientists. However, the same thing should be true of Christians. What is valid in one Christian's experience is corroborated by the experience of other Christians.

One example of scientific evidence is William Pollard's thesis, elaborated on in Chapter 4 of *Physicist and Christian*, that every path of investigation of nature leads to supernature. Many of C. S. Lewis' books (e.g., *Miracles, Mere Christianity*, and *The Abolition of Man*) and Elton Trueblood's (e.g., *A Place to Stand, Philosophy of Religion*, and *General Philosophy*) discuss various types of evidence. Perhaps none of these paths alone is convincing to a given individual, but remember that the same thing was true in the scientific method. As Trueblood makes clear, the power of cumulative evidence is the really important point here.

There are paradoxes in the Biblical model of reality, for example, man's free will and God's sovereignty, God's justice and mercy, and human suffering and God's love. We can't overlook these problems, but paradoxes do not necessarily overthrow the model.[8] There are extremely difficult paradoxes in the mathematical system of real numbers, but all the mathematicians I know have a great deal of faith in it. Physicists cannot reconcile the wave and particle nature of light, but they believe in both. Whether the paradoxes in the Biblical theory of reality are enough to overthrow a person's faith depends upon the strength of the cumulative evidence and the weakness of the alternative models. Atheism, for example, has the problem of trying to answer the questions of how personality can be produced by an impersonal universe or how love and care can come from an unloving and uncaring universe. As Elton Trueblood has said, "A believer believes in God partly because he is unable to make a leap of faith as great as the atheist is forced to make."[9]

H. Gwynne Jones, professor of psychology at Leeds University, in a speech before the Rationalist Press Association said that a hope and belief in the essential goodness of human nature "is not rationally based at all and in fact is belied by most of the evidence in the world today. Nevertheless, I do believe it."[10] In other words, a rationalist must believe in something against all the evidence!

In humanistic determinism, we are asked to believe first of all that man is the result of a completely random evolutionary process and then these random processes in our brain have ultimate meaning, both logically and ethically. Will Durant states the problem of determinism in this way.

Finally, was determinism any more intelligible than free will? If the present moment contains no living and creative choice, and is totally and mechanically the product of the matter and motion of the moment before, then so was that moment the mechanical effort of the moment that preceded it, and that again of the one before…and so on, until we arrive at the primeval nebula as the total cause of every later event, of every line of Shakespeare's plays, and every suffering of his soul, so that the sombre rhetoric of Hamlet and Othello, of MacBeth and Lear, in every clause and every phrase, was written far off there in the distant skies and the distant aeons, by the structure and content of that legendary cloud. What a draft of credulity! What an exercise of faith such a theory must demand in this unbelieving generation! What mystery or miracle, of Old Testament or New, could be half so incredible as this monstrous fatalistic myth, this nebula composing tragedies?[11]

In contrast, Christianity, although it contains paradoxes, is supported by reason. I believe that reason may be very helpful in coming to believe that Christianity is true. However, this is far from the whole story. Jesus gives us a more certain path to truth in His prayer recorded in John 17. There Jesus says that if Christians have the same loving unity that the Father and Son have, then men will know that Jesus came from God and that God loves them. Therefore, there is this one sure proof for Christianity. The love in the Christian community is to be of such a miraculous nature that people will know that a supernatural power is at work. However, this idea needs to be elaborated and we will consider it at greater length in Part II.

C. S. Lewis compared theology with other sciences in the following passage. "Theology is, in a sense, experimental knowledge…like the other experimental sciences in some ways, but not in all."[12] A geologist studying a rock is completely in charge. The rock can do nothing to help or to hinder the investigation. A zoologist studying animals is partly dependent on the behavior of the animals. The initiative is evenly divided between the scientist and the subject of investigation when a psychologist studies another human being. In theology, man's study of God, the initiative lies wholly with God, the subject of investigation. Man can learn nothing about God unless God chooses to reveal Himself. Fortunately, God wants to reveal Himself to all men. God reveals more of Himself to some men than to others and some of His attributes to one and other qualities to someone else. This is not because He has favorites, but because of the condition of individual men. The instrument through which we see God is our complete selves. Just as the image in a dirty telescope is blurred; so if we are not clean, our image of God is blurred. Lewis goes further and says,

> God can show Himself as He really is only to real men. And that means not simply to men who are individually good, but to men who are united together in a body, loving one another, helping one another, showing Him to one another. Consequently, the one really adequate instrument for learning about

God, is the whole Christian community, waiting for Him together. Christian brotherhood is, so to speak, the technical
equipment for this science—the laboratory outfit.[13]
Therefore, it is through the love in a Christian community that unbelievers come to know God and believers learn more about God. As
Kagawa has said, "God is revealed only in Love. He who would hear
the Voice of God should love. Where love is richest, God is best
known."[14] The idea that love may be an aid to knowledge is explored
further in the chapter of Part II entitled "Love and Knowledge."

My conclusion is that the process of understanding and believing
in divine revelation is very much similar to the process of understanding and coming to have a faith in a scientific model. I realize that
revelation must be a gift to us from God, but our evaluation of it and
acceptance of it may be a result of a reasoning process very much like
the scientific method. And, we should remember that scientific models are obtained in various ways, perhaps even sometimes by revelation, but, in any case, they must be checked by the procedures in the
scientific method. In my opinion, we tend to overestimate the role of
reason in science and underestimate the role of reason in religion. As
Quoted earlier, Bertrand Russell, one of the greatest mathematical lo-
gicians, said,

> There is an element of truth to be learned from the mystical
> way of thinking (revelation, insight, intuition) which does not
> seem to be obtained by any other manner+. What I do wish to
> maintain—and it is here that the scientific method is impera-
> tive—is that insight, untested and unsupported is an insuffi-
> cient guarantee of truth, in spite of the fact that much of the
> most important truth is first suggested by its means."[15]

This relationship is stated by the theologian J. Edward Dicks in this
way,

> "Reason can become effective only when it is supplied mate-
> rial that is given it by faith. The relation is one of reciprocity.
> Reason contributes as it makes a critical analysis of faith, tests
> its premises, interrogates its criteria, and holds in check its ten-
> dency to resort to authority.[16]

Perhaps, you were not conscious of this sort of process in your own experience. It is my belief that consciously or unconsciously you used reason in some of the ways I have described. If not, as Pascal has said, "Those to whom God has imparted religion by intuition are very fortunate and justly convinced. But to those who do not have it, we can give it only by reasoning, waiting for God to give spiritual insight, without which faith is only human and useless for salvation."[17] For some people, at least, reason plays an important role in coming to faith. Reason cannot lead a man to God, but it can lead him to a position where God is able to reveal himself to man. Therefore, for many reasons, I agree with J. Edward Dicks' statement that "a faith accepted by critical analysis by reason is better than a faith coddled to avoid contact with reason."[18] Also, I agree with the biochemist Denis Alexander, that "the revelation of God in Christ is accepted because as a general model of explanation it 'fits the facts' about the human condition in a way that no other model does."[19]

Beauty and Truth

"It is more important to have beauty in one's equations than to have them fit experiment."

Paul Dirac

In the last chapter, "aesthetic reasons" was in the list of types of evidence for the truth of Christianity. For many people that may seem strange, so I believe that aesthetics requires a chapter of its own.

As we have noted in an earlier chapter, Copernicus and Kepler believed in the heliocentric theory because of its simplicity, harmony, and beauty, and in spite of apparent contradictions with data. They recognized that its appeal was "aesthetic rather than pragmatic."[1] As Copernicus himself said, "We find, therefore, under this orderly arrangement a wonderful symmetry in the universe, and a definite relation of harmony in the motion and magnitude of the orbs, of a kind that is not possible to obtain in any other way."[2] Kepler said of his theory, "I have attested it as true in my deepest soul and I contemplate its beauty with incredible and ravishing delight."[3]

Likewise, Einstein said that he arrived at the theory of relativity because he was "so firmly convinced of the harmony of the universe."[4] Paul Dirac, winner of the Nobel Prize in Physics in 1933, clarifies the epigraph at the beginning of this chapter by going on to say,

... because the discrepancy may be due to minor features which are not properly taken into account and which will get cleared up with further developments of the theory... It seems that if one is working from the point of view of getting beauty in one's equations and if one has a really sound instinct, one is on the sure line of success.[5]

These are not isolated examples. All great scientists judge theories on an aesthetic as well as pragmatic basis. A recent book, *On Aesthetics in Science*[6], has as its major thesis that aesthetics is a way of knowing. John Keats' statement that "'Beauty is truth, truth beauty,'—that is all ye know on earth, and all ye need to know." goes too far, I believe. Still, beauty seems to be closely related to truth. At the very least, it is not always the case that an ugly fact will kill a beautiful theory. And, the great scientists believe that, usually, the beautiful theory will kill the ugly fact.

It may come as a surprise to some that science or mathematics could be considered beautiful. However mathematics and science are activities

> of creative and imaginative human beings, not of computers or other machines. The creativity and imagination must be controlled by discipline and self-criticism, but that is equally true of other kinds of creative activity such as the writing of poetry. And because it is a creative and imaginative activity, there are satisfactions in engaging in it no different from those felt by creative artists in their work, and there is a beauty in the results that can be enjoyed by others in the same way that poems, pictures, and symphonies are.[7]

The French mathematician Henri Poincare said, "A scientist worthy of the name, above all a mathematician, experiences in his work the same expression as an artist; his pleasure is as great and of the same nature." G. H. Hardy, a British mathematician, agreed, "The mathematician's patterns, like the painter's or the poet's, must be beautiful, the ideas, like the colours or the words, must fit together in a harmonious way. Beauty is the first test: there is no permanent place in the world for ugly mathematics."

Many similar quotations could be given, but I would like to be able to show the reader some examples instead. However, this is not an easy thing to do. There is beauty in geometric design that all have experienced and that is part of the beauty of mathematics, but not the most important part. As Hardy said, it is ideas in mathematics that must fit together as colors, words, or musical notes do in other areas. Just as it takes some musical development to properly appreciate a Bach fugue, so it takes some mathematical development to appreciate group theory. Still, I would like to try to give you a taste of beauty in mathematics, frustrating as it may be to you and to me.

The ancient Greeks believed that a rectangle whose ratio of length to width was (approx. 1.618) was the most pleasing to the eye. Whether or not this is true, artists have used it in many ways from the Parthenon in Athens to Dali's "The Last Supper." This rectangle is called the golden rectangle. For me its beauty lies in something more than its visual appearance. For example, if a square is taken off of one side of the golden rectangle, what is left is a smaller rectangle with the same ratio of length to width, that is, another golden rectangle. Therefore, one can take a square away from it again and again, ad infinitum. (See Fig. 7-1.) If ABCD is a golden rectangle and AFED is a square, then FBCE is a golden rectangle and so on.

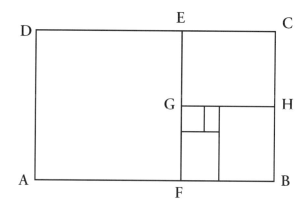

Figure 7-1.

Now this infinite progression has a mystery and beauty that I enjoy as I do the contemplation of any beautiful object. But this is just the beginning. If one draws in diagonals and then replaces the diagonals by smooth curves, one obtains a lovely spiral. (See Fig. 7-2.) These spirals occur often in nature, for example the shell of the chambered nautilus and the arrangement of seeds in a sunflower. Surprisingly, this golden ratio, $\frac{1 + \sqrt{5}}{2}$, appears often in a regular pentagon, first as the ratio of a diagonal to a side. Then, if all of the diagonals are drawn, a star is formed and another pentagon appears in the center, so again, the process can be imagined to continue infinitely. (See Fig. 7-3.) Now the golden ratio appears over and over, and not just in the ratio of diagonals to sides, but in other pairs of line segments and even pairs of areas.

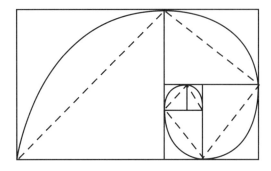

Figure 7-2.

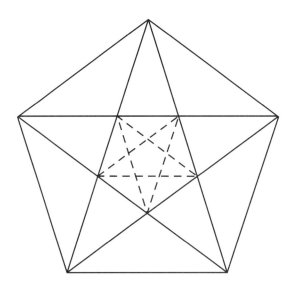

Figure 7-3.

And we have just scratched the surface of the many relationships that come from the golden ratio. It occurs in three-dimensional objects like the Platonic solids. Then it also occurs in connection with the

Fibonacci sequence of numbers (1, 1, 2, 3, 5, 8,…) and the Fibonacci numbers occur, again seemingly miraculously, in many places from the genealogy of a male bee to the placement of leaves along the stems of plants and the number of spirals in a sunflower. Here is where the frustration comes in. I would like to give you a two-hour lecture, complete with three dimensional models, slides, and overheads, but since I can't right now, I hope this brief introduction to the golden rectangle will give you a glimpse into the beauty of ideas in mathematics. And this is only one small example.

To a mathematician, beauty appears everywhere in mathematics. Concerning the difficulty of conveying to others why these things are beautiful, one of the greatest of living mathematicians, Paul Erdos, said, "It's like asking why Beethoven's Ninth Symphony is beautiful. If you don't see why, someone can't tell you. I know numbers are beautiful. If they aren't beautiful, nothing is."[8] Mathematicians are not the only people who recognize beauty in mathematics. The poet Edna St. Vincent Millay said,

"O blinding light, O holy terrible day,
When first the shaft into his vision shone
Of light anatomized! Euclid alone
Has looked on beauty bare."

Even though I cannot explain what beauty is, in mathematics, science, or anywhere else, I know when I recognize and enjoy it, and I believe that it must have a significance. It must tell us something about the universe and the Creator. Perhaps these patterns in mathematics must necessarily exist and so tell us nothing about the nature of the Creator. Yet, the fact that man is such a being that can appreciate that order, simplicity and harmony must tell us something about the Creator. Just as the beautiful colors of a sunset might be a necessary physical phenomenon, still we might all be color blind and not be able to appreciate it. The fact that all of us are able to "see" beauty somewhere, if not in mathematics, then in nature, art, music, or elsewhere, does suggest a loving Creator.

Going back to our old friends, Copernicus and Kepler, we find that they believed that theories in astronomy should be beautiful. As they discovered more of that beauty it gave evidence of the existence and nature of God.

> Kepler was so moved that he wrote,
> The wisdom of the Lord is infinite; so also are His glory and His power. Ye heavens, sing His praises! Sun, moon, and planets glorify Him in your ineffable language! Celestial harmonies, all ye who comprehend His marvelous works, praise Him, and thou, my soul, praise the Creator! It is by Him and in Him that all exists. That which we know best is comprised in Him, as well as in our vain science. To Him be praise, honor, and glory throughout eternity.[9]

Isaac Newton, in a book on optics, asked a series of questions and then gave the answer.

> What is there in places almost empty of matter, and whence is it that the sun and planets gravitate towards one another, without dense matter between them? Whence is it that nature doth nothing in vain; and whence arises all that order and beauty we see in the world? To what end are comets, . . . what hinders the fixed stars from falling upon one another? How came the bodies of animals to be contrived with so much art, and for what ends were their several parts? Was the eye contrived without skill in optics, or the ear without knowledge of sounds? How do the motions of the body follow from the will, and whence is the instinct in animals?…And these things being rightly dispatched, does it not appear from phenomena that there is a being incorporeal, living, intelligent, omnipresent, who, in infinite space, as it were in his sensory, sees the things themselves intimately, and thoroughly perceives them; and comprehends them wholly by their immediate presence to himself?[10]

In Newton's magnus opus, the *Principia*, he asserts, "This most beautiful system of sun, planets, and comets could only proceed from the counsel and dominion of an intelligent and powerful Being… This Being governs all things, not as the soul of the world, but Lord over all."[11]

The belief has continued in many of the great scientists into the twentieth century. Paul Dirac said God used beautiful mathematics to create the world, "Beautiful but not simple. My theories are based on a faith that there is a reason for all the numbers nature provides us with." The astronomer Hugh Ross wrote,

> The beauty principle is the presupposition that the correct description of nature is that which manifests the greatest degree of simplicity, beauty, elegance, and consistency. So far this principle has been an unerring guide to new insights in theoretical physics. It also is a statement about who or what created the universe.[12]

Mathematicians and scientists are not the only people to see the connection between beauty and knowledge of God. Someone once asked Gandhi, is there Truth in a sunset or a crescent moon that shines amid the stars at night?" And we might add, in the beauty of a mathematical theory. Gandhi's answer was,

> Indeed, these beauties are truthful inasmuch as they make me think of the Creator at the back of them. How could these be beautiful but for the Truth that is in the centre of creation. When I admire the wonder of a sunset or the beauty of the moon, my soul expands in worship of the Creator. I try to see Him and His mercies in all these creations. But even the sunsets and sunrises would be mere hindrances if they did not help me think of Him.[13]

Tagore, the Indian poet, said, "Somewhere in the arrangement of this world there seems to be a great concern about giving us delight, which shows that, in the universe, over and above the meaning of matter and forces, there is a message conveyed through the magic touch of personality."

The existence of beauty in this world does not prove that Christianity is true or even that there is a God. However, just as beauty is used by scientists as a path to truth, so it may be supporting evidence for the Christian hypothesis. As Elton Trueblood has said, "If the world is the creation of Infinite Mind, the prodigious beauty of the world makes sense. In short, if theism is true, the aesthetic experience of natural beauty is what we should expect to find."[14]

Imagination and Reality

*"The moving power of mathematical invention
is not reasoning but imagination."*

Augustus DeMorgan

"What is now proved was once only imagined."

William Blake

Probably to most people, the word "imagination" conveys the idea of unreality. However, imaginary does not necessarily mean unreal. Imagination is the act or power of forming mental images. Mental images may or may not be closely related to reality. It is the role of reason to determine that relationship. It may seem as though science deals with facts, hard data, or little chunks of reality. Actually all "facts" have been experienced through one or more of our senses and so are more or less distorted. Furthermore, they are colored by mental constructs already existing in our minds. That is, we automatically force them to fit the models of reality that we have consciously or unconsciously already accepted. It is only when we have great trouble fitting the facts into our present models that our imagination attempts to find a better model. Whether or not the new model is better can only be determined by reason and experience.

The twentieth-century mathematician Herman Weyl said, "Science would perish without a supporting transcendental faith in truth and reality, and without the continuous interplay between its facts and constructions on the one hand and the imagery of ideas on the other."[1] The philosopher of science Karl Popper has said that we can achieve knowledge "because we can invent myths, stories, theories; because we have a thirst for explanations, an insatiable curiosity, a wish to know. Because we not only invent stories and theories, but try them out and see whether they work and how they work... [for example] by making up a myth about 'invisibles' such as atoms or gravitational forces which explain the visible."[2] He goes on to say, "I doubt if there is much to choose here between science and the arts: The imagination is not much more free, and not much less free, in one than in the other."[3]

In mathematics and science, as in any other area, the life-giving force is imagination, controlled imagination. As we have seen, we must have imaginative constructs that then must be tested by reason and experience. One writer goes so far as to say that imagination is "an actual extra sense with which we can perceive the natural world. And it is an extremely efficacious sense, because it often perceives reality long before our scientific senses do."[4] If true, this would account for the fact that the imaginative constructions of mathematics have been so surprisingly effective in applications. If imagination were no more than a random process in our brains, mathematics could not have as many applications as it has. For example, why should the mathematically beautiful ellipse, which was invented by the Greeks about 2,000 years ago, describe the paths of planets? Or, why should a non-Euclidean geometry developed by Riemann be applicable fifty years later in the theory of relativity? Some say we have this sense because our minds and nature have developed from the same evolutionary process. I think a better explanation would be that our imaginative sense was created by the same God who created the rest of nature.

On the other hand, if imagination is a sixth sense, why is it that so many other creations of the human imagination seemingly have no correspondence in the real world (e.g. unicorns, fauns, and hobbits, although even these may tell us something about reality). These could, of course, just be aberrations of that sixth sense. After all, our five senses have aberrations also. Perhaps because of the Fall, this creative sense fell more than our other senses. The idea that imagination is a sixth sense is itself a product of imagination and so could be incorrect. In any case, controlled imagination is a powerful force in helping us to understand the real world.

Mathematics is a set of imaginative constructs that is not reality but may be a helpful representation of reality. It comes from the interaction of experience, imagination, intuition, and revelation, "sifted, refined, and organized by the logic men are willing and able to apply at any time."[5]

I believe this sheds some light on the nature of existence in mathematics, that is, on the question of what kind of existence numbers or lines (for example) possess. I remember that during a discussion period at a conference on the relation between mathematics and Christianity, someone suggested that mathematical entities exist in the same sense that the Narnian characters like Aslan and Reepicheep exist. That is, mathematical and literary existence are the same. I believe there is some truth in that. An author is creatively building concepts having some relationship to reality. We hope that the correspondence is much closer with mathematics. However, Tolkien did believe he was discovering and exploring Middle Earth rather than creating it ex nihilo.

Thus, mathematics is not entirely different from other human endeavors. In fact, as we have seen, it is very closely related to science. The difference is that in mathematics we concentrate more on the deductive development of the postulates than the scientist does, while the scientist is more concerned about how closely the model corresponds to reality than the mathematician is. However, neither can completely ignore the other part very long without great peril. Even a poet is concerned, in his own way, with the same process.

Perhaps it is time to take a closer look at the origin of postulates in mathematics. Do they come from experience of reality, intuition of reality, or are they creative constructs of our imagination perhaps not even related to the "real" world? That is, is mathematics a creation of someone's mind or is it a discovery of something that exists in the real world? I would have to answer, "It is both a discovery and a creation." It is out of experience with reality that mathematical concepts arise. So in that sense, we discover. But, remember that our view of reality comes through several filters so that what our mind creates may not be exactly what is out there waiting to be discovered. However, by elaborating the consequences of our creation, we may discover much more about the real world. And remember, as Tycho said, we needed some hypothesis before we could look at the facts in the first place. It seems as though we need data before we can create concepts and hypotheses, but we need hypotheses and concepts before we can assimilate data. Each must come before the other!

Returning to mathematic's parallel with literature consider that Tolkien made certain creative assumptions about orcs, dwarves, elves, and hobbits, and then he discovered the implications of those assumptions. But in some sense, those creative assumptions came from his experience and understanding of reality. Of course, his assumptions were never stated as explicitly as they are in mathematics. Still, the interplay between creativity and discovery, between imagination and reality in literature is similar to the process in mathematics.

There are times when our imaginations need to be stretched so that we can have even the possibility of comprehending reality; times when the imaginative constructs of the past are inadequate for the present and our minds are not yet capable of creating the necessary new constructs. For example, before geometry could begin, someone had to imagine a straight line. Geometrical lines do not exist in the real world. Our closest approximations of a line are not perfectly straight and must have three dimensions even if two of the dimensions are very small. A geometrical line having only one dimension could not be seen. Thus, the concept had to come from someone's imagination. Then it could be used to help us understand the real world. Euclidean geometry has certainly helped us to do that.

The development of non-Euclidean geometry illustrates the role of imagination in mathematics. From the time of Euclid, mathematicians puzzled over the fact that his Parallel Postulate seemed to demand a proof. That is, it was not as "self-evident" as the rest of his postulates and axioms and therefore should be proved. Then in the mid-nineteenth century several mathematicians, Gauss, Bolya, and Lobachevsky, had imaginations powerful enough to conceive of the possibility that instead of being provable it might even be false. Some other mathematicians, Saccheri, for example, had studied the problem just as much or possibly more than Gauss, Bolya, and Lobachevsky, but their minds did not make the necessary imaginative leap and so were unable to develop non-Euclidean geometries. Other imaginative minds constructed various kinds of models to help us understand non-Euclidean geometries and others developed them. These geometries helped to stretch men's minds and within a half century Einstein used one of them as a basis for a new model of reality, his theory of relativity.

In the area of religion, also, we often need to have our imaginations expanded, as J.B. Phillips reminds us in his book *Your God Is Too Small.* Writers like Tolkien, Lewis, and Williams are excellent for expanding our minds, making us aware of new possibilities, and helping us to make sense out of paradoxes in Christianity. For example, God's sovereignty and man's freedom have successfully defied man's attempt to describe them in words. I believe that Lewis' imagination can take us a little further toward understanding those concepts through his description of the struggle between good and evil on the unfallen planet, *Perelandra,* and through the experiences of some of the bus travelers from the gray city in *The Great Divorce.*

Another reason why imagination is important is that it allows us to have knowledge of truth that exceeds propositional truth. Human language is finite. Some of us have more trouble with it than others, but even for the best of us it is finite. God is infinite, so finite human language can not describe God completely in propositional form. And of course, we are finite, so there is no way we can completely comprehend God. But through imaginative constructions we may be able to apprehend some reality about God that we are unable to put into propositions. As C. S. Lewis has said, a story may do "what no theorem can quite do. It may not be [like real life] in the superficial sense: but it sets before us an image of what reality may well be like at some more central region."[6]

Imaginative constructs in one area often affect workers in some other area. For example, the mathematical concept of infinity inspired an intriguing series of prints by M.C. Escher attempting to capture the idea of infinity on a finite two-dimensional sheet. Poincare's Model for Lobachevskian geometry was used in at least one of these prints. This kind of cross fertilization is not one way. In fact, it is sometimes hard to tell which form of culture is influencing and which is being influenced.

For example, has the concept of an infinite God affected the concept of infinity in mathematics, or vice versa, or both? Another example is the mathematical concept of the fourth dimension, which may be used to illustrate many ideas in religion and will be more fully described in the next chapter.

Exactly what this power of imagination consists of is beyond the scope of this book because it is beyond the scope of its author. It is affected by experience and reason, and it is my belief that divine revelation may be involved and that some things may be implanted in all human minds by God, that is, by some kind of basic programming. In fact, at the point in Genesis (Chapter 1, verse 27) where we are told that man was created in the image of God, about the only thing that had previously been described about God was his creative activity. This has led some people to claim that the primary attribute man possesses by virtue of being made in the image of God is creativity. Although I believe that ability to create is not the primary attribute, I do believe that one of the things we have because of God's image in us is imagination.

However that may be and whatever else may be involved in the process of imagining, imagination does exist. Mental images of various kinds do come somehow into our minds, and it is the duty of our reason to make a judgment about their relation to reality. We never have the choice between reality and imagination, only between various products of our imagination. Of course, the models we use are not solely the product of our own imagination. Someone else may suggest a model for us to consider. But, no matter how explicitly someone describes a model to us, it must in some way become a construct in our own minds and hence in that way a product of our own imagination.

As we have seen, science, mathematics, and religion consist of experience and products of imagination tested by reason and experience. That is, after imagination constructs models of reality, then reason and experience choose the most satisfying model for us to live by. Perhaps the best thing for us to do now is to consider one product of man's imagination, the idea of a fourth dimension of space, its usefulness in understanding reality, and the role of reason in the whole process.

A Fourth Dimension

"All three of us knew, and Ransom had actually experienced,
how thin is the crust which protects 'real life' from the fantastic."
. . . from "The Dark Tower" by C. S. Lewis

One of the ways in which imagination comes into play in science is a creative mind taking bits of information and putting them together in a new and ingenious way to make a model of reality that seems to fit our experience better than any previous model. Often, these bits of information have been available to many, but it took the imagination of a genius to synthesize them, thus bringing into being the new model.

But there are also times, especially in mathematics, when someone extrapolates imaginatively from the known into the unknown for the sheer joy of mental construction, without even a suspicion of applicability. Going from the known to the unknown is always risky, partly because the known never points unequivocally the direction in which to travel. This may be illustrated by infinite sequences of numbers. An infinite sequence is just an unending string of numbers. An example would be 1,4,9,16,25, … with the three dots indicating that it continues forever in the way it has started. Now what I had in mind in that example was a sequence consisting of squares of whole numbers, that is the nth term is n^2. Thus, although I can't write down all the numbers in the sequence, I can tell you what any particular one is. For example, if you ask for the 40th term, I can tell you that it is 1600.

Now let us consider an infinite sequence of numbers which begins with 2 and 4. Someone might logically suggest that the first six terms of that sequence are 2,4,6,8,10,12. Someone else with a little more imagination but just as much logic might suggest 2,4,8,16,32,64. The first six terms might really be 2,4,4,2,-2,-8. Actually, there are many possibilities.[1] The point is that when one extrapolates from the known into the unknown, it is possible to go in the wrong direction. Still, one obtains new ideas that reason can evaluate.

An important example of this process occurred in geometry. On any straight line, if one point is chosen and labeled 0 and any other point (usually one slightly to the right of the one labeled 0) is labeled 1, then a one-to-one correspondence is set up between the point on the line and the set of real numbers. (See Figure 9-1.)

-2	$-\dfrac{3}{2}$	-1	$-\dfrac{1}{2}$	0	$\dfrac{1}{2}$	1	$\dfrac{3}{2}$	2	$\dfrac{5}{2}$	3

Figure 9-1.

Similarly, we can use two lines at right angles to each other, to set up a one-to-one correspondence between points in the plane and the set of ordered pairs of real numbers. (See Figure 9-2.) The first number locates the points relative to the horizontal line, while the second number indicates its relation to the vertical line.

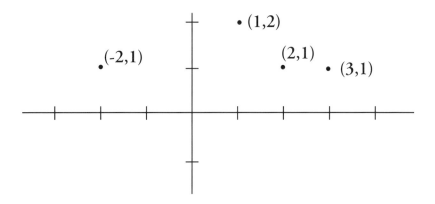

Figure 9-2.

Now, by using three lines at right angles to each other, we can set up a one-to-one correspondence between points in space and ordered triples of real numbers, each of the three numbers giving its position relative to one of the three lines. (See Figure 9-3.)

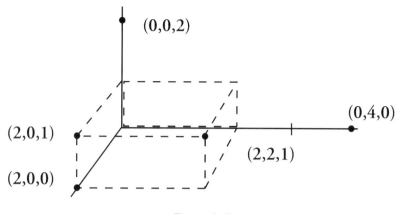

Figure 9-3.

This process of assigning numbers to points in space is called analytic geometry and is very useful since it relates the algebra of real numbers to geometry, the geometry of the line, the geometry of the plane and the geometry of space, respectively. It allows us on the one hand to use algebra to study geometry when that is helpful, and on the other hand to use geometry to picture algebraic relations. It is not necessary to describe in detail how analytic geometry has been beneficial. Suffice it to say that it has led to calculus and innumerable applications in physics, all of natural science, and even the social sciences.

This method of combining geometry with numbers or algebra occurred to two of the great mathematicians of all time, Rene Descartes and Pierre Fermat, almost simultaneously. But the imaginative leap that gave us analytic geometry, as important as it is, is not what I want to discuss now. The next step is what I want to talk about. And that is, considering four lines each at right angles to all of the rest, we should have a one-to-one correspondence between that geometry and ordered quadruples of real numbers. Now if you really tried to consider what I suggested in the last sentence, you must have had a problem. If you didn't have a problem with it, that is, if you could visualize four lines at right angles to each other, I wish you would contact me immediately! Although this next logical step in algebra is very easy since ordered quadruples of numbers cause no difficulties (e.g. (2,5,1,7) or (8,3,9,0)), it is humanly impossible to conceive of four mutually perpendicular lines.

Even though our intuition seems to be limited to a space of three dimensions, this did not keep mathematicians from creating in their imaginations a four-dimensional geometry. By analogy from two and three dimensions, they could make some assumptions about four and use reason to develop it. Reason is not restricted to three dimensions, or for that matter, to four. So mathematicians have had great fun building five, six, and even infinite-dimensional geometries. It would seem that these creations were purely imaginary with no relation at all to reality. However that may be, they were valuable to mathematics. By using reason in these different situations, these mathematicians contributed to our insight into the reasoning process and even though the geometries were strange they did contribute to the corresponding algebra. So higher dimensional geometries became an important part of mathematics.[2]

The really surprising thing about these new geometries is that physicists applied them. Einstein found that a four-dimensional geometry developed by the German mathematician Bernhard Riemann had precisely the right characteristics to be used in his theory of relativity to explain gravity. As physicist William G. Pollard, Executive Director of the Oak Ridge Institute of Nuclear Studies and an Episcopal priest, relates it, "How planets move or how gravity behaves had not the slightest influence on Riemann in the development of his geometry. Only the human mind and imagination were involved in that development."[3] Perhaps even more surprising is the application of an infinite- dimensional geometry developed by David Hilbert with no idea of any connection with the real world. Physicists have used Hilbert's geometry to describe "accurately all the properties of atomic nuclei, atoms, molecules, and crystalline solids."[4]

One other contribution of higher dimensional geometries is the way they stretch our imaginations, expand our horizons (I wonder what horizons are like in a space of five dimensions!), and make us aware of new possibilities, in much the same way that Lewis' space trilogy does, and thus aid us in a new and deeper understanding and appreciation of reality. The best way I know to help you understand that last statement is to use the device employed by Edwin A. Abbott in his classic book *Flatland.* Approximately a century ago, Abbott, a schoolmaster with primary interests in literature and theology, wrote a captivating story about spaces of various dimensions.

Abbot created a fictional universe called Flatland, which was a completely flat universe something like the top of a table or a perfectly level floor. In this universe there are creatures of various, more or less regular, shapes: triangles, squares, other polygons, and even circles. They are capable of movement, rational thought, emotions and other human-like characteristics. They live in houses that appear like floor plans to us looking down on them. Many questions could be raised (some of which could be answered) concerning these creatures, which need not be considered for our purposes. The main thing we must keep in mind is that they are completely restricted to two dimensions. They have no experience and no conception of a third dimension.

One of these creatures, a square, is alone in his study with the door closed. Incidentally, he is a mathematician. He feels secure within his four walls and has no idea that we can look down on him in his room. We can, in fact, see inside of him as well as the inside of his room. (See Figure 9-4.)

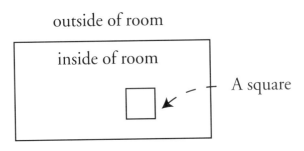

Figure 9-4.

Suddenly, in the closed room, the square is shocked to see a small circle appear and grow larger. From our vantage point we can see that a sphere has dropped into his room from the third dimension. The sphere tries to make the square understand that he is a sphere and not just a circle with a variable radius. The square, having no concept of a third dimension, cannot understand the sphere at all. Finally, in desperation, the sphere snatches the square and drags him out of his plane into the third dimension.

Then the square can look back on Flatland, and through a long conversation with the sphere, can understand the nature of three-dimensional space. Recently, it seems providentially, the square had had a dream about Lineland, a one-dimensional universe, in which creatures were limited to a line. So the square can use the process of going from one dimension to two as an analogy to help him in going from two to three. For example, in his dream he dropped into the line from his two dimensional world, but to the Linelanders he appeared to be a line segment, just as the sphere had appeared to him to be only a circle.

Finally, in their conversation, the square announces that he has mastered this step and is ready to move on to a higher dimension. Now it is the sphere's turn to be confused: he knows nothing of a fourth dimension and insists that there is none. The square having made the difficult transition from his native two dimensions into three can readily imagine a fourth and even higher order dimensions, but the sphere cannot. The sphere can make nothing of the square's argument for a fourth dimension and eventually deposits the square back in Flatland. Now the square has the unenviable, and in fact, impossible task of convincing his fellow Flatlanders of the existence of a third dimension. He seems compelled to try. He ends up in solitary confinement. If you are interested in learning more about Flatland and the square's adventure, I heartily recommend that you read the book.[5]

Perhaps I should tell you about one of the square's devices or ideas for understanding higher dimensions. I do this for two reasons, one to give an idea of how these analogies might work and because we will use this particular one later. Figure 9-5 should be helpful in following this discussion.

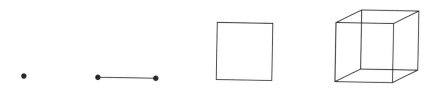

Figure 9-5.

First, there is only one zero-dimensional object, a point. In a line, if you take two of these points or zero-dimensional objects and join them, you get a one-dimensional object, a line segment. In a plane, if you take two of these line segments or one-dimensional objects and join their endpoints, you get a two-dimensional object, a square. In space, if you take two of these squares or two-dimensional objects and join their vertices, you get a three-dimensional object, a cube. "Now," said the square, "if you take two cubes in the space of four dimensions, you get a four-dimensional object." Although the square did not know its name, mathematicians call this hypothetical four- dimensional analogue of a cube a tesseract or a hypercube. Figure 9-5 does not contain a drawing of a tesseract because a two-dimensional (which is what a sheet of paper is) model of the fourth dimension gets quite complicated (see front cover). I do have a three-dimensional model of a tesseract in my office. It was easy to make out of sticks. It just takes two cubes with their vertices connected. We will return to a discussion of these figures later. For anyone interested in learning more about this subject, I would recommend the books *The Fourth Dimension Simply Explained*[6], edited by Henry P. Manning and *The Fourth Dimension* by Rudy Rucker.[7] The Manning book is a collection of essays in response to a request from the journal "The Scientific American." Regardless of how much the mathematics of the fourth dimension is developed or even applied, the status of its existence is described by Manning in this way:

> Even a workable hypothesis based on the existence of four-dimensional space, though it might serve temporarily better than any other hypothesis, would hardly justify a belief in this existence. But we do say that the existence of space of four dimensions can never be disproved by showing that it is absurd or inconsistent; for such is not the case. Nor, on the other hand, will the most elaborate development of the analogues of different kinds ever prove that it does exist.[8]

In other words, no matter how interesting and useful the idea of a fourth dimension is we will never know if it is true and, on the other hand, no matter how strange and opposed to our intuition it is, we will never know that it is false.

In *The Dialogues* (Book VII) Plato has Socrates tell of a group of people who are chained in a cave. They are facing a wall and cannot look behind them. There is a fire behind them, so that all they can see are shadows on the wall of the cave. As a student in *The Dialogues* says, the truth for these people would be literally nothing but the shadows. Now shadows, of course, are only two-dimensional. Therefore, reality for these three-dimensional beings has been restricted to two dimensions. Perhaps we are four, or higher-dimensional beings restricted to three-dimensional experience.

We have already seen that higher-dimensional geometry is profitable in understanding nuclear physics. Pollard describes how, shortly after World War II, it was thought that matter could be adequately described in terms of protons, neutrons, and electrons. Then it was discovered that they are in turn made up of a throng (or rabble) of other particles, which in turn may be made up of very elusive particles called quarks. It begins to appear as though when, if ever, we get to the very heart of matter we will find, not matter, but simply mathematical properties. As Pollard says, "Like Plato's famous cave, the whole material universe in three-dimensional space and time with all its seeming substantiality may be at heart made up of mere shadows of realities which transcend space and time and so are inaccessible to our direct observation."[9] If this is right, then truth is, for us in this life, nothing but the three-dimensional shadow of reality.

As we have seen, when we extrapolate from the known to the unknown, we must be careful. I'm not sure what the mathematicians who first looked into the fourth dimension were looking for, and so I don't know if they found whatever it was they were anticipating. However, if they didn't find what they were looking for, it seems that they found something better. Our imaginations may not help us find what we were looking for. We may find something better, or perhaps worse, or maybe nothing at all. However, it is certain that if we don't look at all, we will find nothing. In the next chapter we will investigate some possible implications of all of this to our understanding of Christianity.

Higher Dimensions and Christianity

"Spacelanders of moderate and modest minds
who—speaking of that which is of highest importance,
but lies beyond experience—decline to say on the one
hand, 'This can never be,' and on the other hand, 'It
must needs be precisely thus, and we know all about it.'"

Edwin A. Abbott

In this chapter it would be easy for the reader to misunderstand what I am trying to do, so I feel that it is important to say a few things at the beginning to clarify my intentions. In science when a new theory or model is suggested, it is tentatively assumed to be true and its implications are deduced and tested against reality. If it agrees with the available data better than any other model, it is accepted until a better model emerges. Therefore, I would like to explore the hypothesis that reality is four-dimensional or higher to see how it fits in with various incidents in the Bible and aspects of Christian theology that have been difficult for some people to understand. As I pointed out in the last chapter, none of this can prove that there is a fourth dimension. My belief in God does not depend on this "explanation" of events. I believe that God is powerful enough to accomplish things in ways I cannot and need not comprehend. Still, it may be of help to some to see how man's mind can devise models to explain some things. The purpose, then, of this chapter is to stretch your imaginations. And if this is not the correct explanation, then the real explanation, which we may know some day, will, in all probability, be more fantastic and much more beautiful.

As a first consideration of a possible fourth space dimension to aid in our understanding of the Bible, consider John 20:26: "The doors were shut, but Jesus came and stood among them, and said, 'Peace be with you.'" John makes it clear that the doors were shut. It was not that the disciples were preoccupied and did not notice Jesus walking through the door. The doors were shut and his appearance was a great surprise.

It was necessary for Jesus to calm their fears by saying, "Peace be with you." Now just as it was easy for the sphere to enter the square's closed room through the third dimension, if there is a fourth dimension, it would be easy for Jesus to move into their room from that dimension. Since this is our first example, let me emphasize again that this idea of dimensions is just one possible explanation. There are many more that man's mind could invent, so imagine what God's mind can do. Perhaps the most common explanation without using a higher dimension is that spirits are less solid and can therefore move through a wall. A more likely possibility is that Jesus was more real and more solid than the wall, the walls being so insubstantial compared with the reality of Jesus that they were no impediment for Him at all. This idea relates rather well to our fourth dimension hypothesis when we remember how substantial three-dimensional objects (we call them solids) are in comparison to two-dimensional objects. For a four-dimensional being, three-dimensional objects would be as insubstantial as plane figures are to us.

In Luke 4, the crowd became angry with Jesus for something He said and took Him out of the city to a cliff and were going to throw Him over. "But passing through the midst of them He went away" (Luke 4:30). Again, there are many possible explanations, but one is that he simply moved into the fourth dimension. Remember how the sphere moved into and out of Flatland at will. Another time the Jews were infuriated with Jesus "so they took up stones to throw at him; but Jesus hid himself, and went out of the temple" (John 8:59). Somehow I can't imagine Jesus ducking into a closet with Peter standing unobtrusively outside and later whispering, "Psst, Peter, are they gone yet?" On the other hand, it seems reasonable to me that Jesus would move off into a different dimension that was as natural a direction to Him as north or south is to us. John 10:39 tells about a similar incident.

The ascension of Jesus is described in Acts 1. "He was lifted up, and a cloud took him out of their sight. And while they were gazing into heaven as he went, behold, two men stood by them in white robes."

Just before this took place, Jesus was likely surrounded by his disciples. If our fourth dimension hypothesis is correct, the disciples would probably have noticed some movement and then could no longer see Him. It was as though a cloud covered Him. He was gone. A horizontal movement would have been in their line of sight, and they did not observe that. Besides, they surrounded Him. He couldn't have moved horizontally. A movement into the earth would not even have occurred to them, so they stared up into the air to try to see where He had gone. They must have been looking in the wrong direction because suddenly (remember the "behold") two men appeared in their three-dimensional world.

Revelation 1:7 says that when Jesus returns, "every eye will see him." Some critics have said that this is an example of the incredibility of the Bible. They charge that John's statement comes from his belief that the earth was flat, which would enable all people on the earth to see Him coming down from the sky. However, since the earth is spherical, there is no way every eye could see Jesus coming because some would have to be on the other side of the earth from Him. Suppose the Flatlanders had been told that someday a god would come and every eye would see him coming. The scoffers would say, "Impossible! There would be houses and forests and all kinds of objects that would interfere with at least some people's ability to see him." But we can conceive of their instantaneously receiving the ability to see into the third dimension and thus being able to observe the coming of a god from that direction. So if we should be able to see the fourth dimension, we could all observe Jesus' return at the same time.

In II Kings 6, the King of Aram sent his army to surround Elisha's house and capture him. Elisha's servant went out in the morning, saw the army, and was afraid. Elisha, however, was not at all afraid. He saw "the hills full of horses and chariots of fire" surrounding the army of the king of Aram. Then he prayed that God would open his servants eyes so he could see them also. Is it possible that angels in chariots of fire were right there, but in the fourth dimension?

In another Biblical story, Daniel's three friends in the furnace may have gone right out of it into a fourth dimension where the fire could not harm them. The manna that the Israelites received in the wilderness, the widow's oil (in the Elisha story), and the loaves and fishes with which Jesus fed the multitude may have come from the forth dimension. I sometimes wonder if there isn't a leak into the fourth dimension from my home with a steady stream of ball point pens going into it!

Another interesting fourth dimension possibility is surgery without incisions. Imagine that our friend from Flatland, the square, develops a tumor that must be removed. Surgeons would have to perform an incision on one of his four sides to remove it. But his friend, the sphere, could easily take it out through the third dimension without disturbing any of his sides. Likewise, God could operate on us from the fourth dimension with no incision. This could be how Jesus performed some of his miracles. I am not trying to "explain away" Jesus' miracles. I believe that He did supernatural things, but He did them in some way that was natural to Him. A fourth dimension is as supernatural to me as anything could be. For me, considering higher dimensions takes nothing away from the power of God. It makes it even more awesome. Remember, if this "explanation" is not the correct one, then something even more wonderful is.

One of the criticisms of Christianity is that the three-layered model of reality (see Figure 10-1) is outmoded and therefore the alleged reality it is supposed to model must not be true.

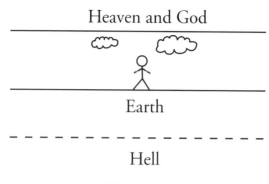

Figure 10-1.

In this model, man walks on the earth, the middle layer; hell is the lower level; and God in heaven is just above man, transcendent but immanent, close enough to have personal contact with man. However, as science expands our knowledge of the universe, God is pushed farther and farther away. Thus, the critics argue, God can no longer be immanent. In a crude form of the argument, the Russian astronaut said he did not find God in outer space. In this form the argument is not very telling for most people, but in a subtle way this has eroded for many the credibility of the Biblical concept of a God who is in personal contact with each of us.

If we again translate this concept and argument to Flatland, we can give some valuable insight. Figure 10-1 was meant to be a two-dimensional picture of three-dimensional reality. For example, the line labeled Earth in the picture was meant to represent a plane. But let us change our point of view and consider Figure 10-1 to actually be a part of Flatland. Now as scientists in Flatland learn more and more about their plane, God is pushed farther and farther away. Critics begin to say that God can no longer be concerned with man. He is too far away. But if their God is three-dimensional, we can see how He can be intimately associated with their "inmost parts." In the same way, if God is four-dimensional, He can be in intimate contact with us at all times precisely because He transcends our puny three dimensions. Thus, God's transcendence and immanence, instead of posing a paradox, are a unity. God is immanent because He is transcendent. William Pollard, the physicist and Anglican priest, suggested reading Psalm 139 in the light of these ideas.

Therefore, the fact that the three layer model is outmoded does not destroy the reality that it attempted to picture. The Bohr model of the atom is outmoded in physics, but physicists have definitely not decided that what it modeled is not real. They have just devised better models. Thus, the fourth dimension is a better model than the old three-layered one. Good scientists do not confuse the model with reality. The model is neither true nor false; it is only better or worse as a tool for understanding reality. So the fourth dimension as a model need not be true to be useful in comprehending spiritual realities.

I am indebted to C. S. Lewis (again) for this next idea concerning the fourth dimension, which I believe may be the most profound and the most useful. Perhaps to be most profound is to be most useful. In any case, consider trying to explain to an unbeliever your conversion, the leading of the Holy Spirit in your life, or any other spiritual experience. If the unbeliever is a good psychologist, he can explain your experience in psychological terms only. He needs no assumptions of the spiritual realm (or dimension) at all. If he is a good physiologist, he can explain it on a purely biological level. Even, if we could find a good enough chemist or physicist, he could explain it on a chemical or physical basis. For some, this has cast doubt on the authenticity of the original spiritual experience.

If the "spiritual" experience can be totally explained on a psychological level then perhaps it is not real. Let us assume for the moment that it can be explained in this way. So the psychologist assumes that it is <u>nothing but</u> a psychological experience. But now the physiologist enters the argument and says that it is not a spiritual experience; it is <u>nothing but</u> a biological experience. Notice that now the psychologist has a problem also. His "psychological" experience is <u>nothing but</u> a biological one. Donald MacKay, a specialist in brain physiology, has called this the fallacy of "nothing buttery." Even if an event can be completely described at one level, Dr. MacKay says that that does not preclude its reality on another level. It is here that our knowledge of dimensions can come to our aid.

If you were to see a tesseract and were told that it was a model of a four-dimensional object, you would almost certainly say that it seems suspicious that it is simply made up of three-dimensional objects. (In the previous chapter a tesseract was described as two cubes with corresponding vertices connected.) A four-dimensional being might respond to your arguments saying, "Of course it must consist of only three-dimensional objects because that is all you understand." That reply may not be satisfying to us, but ponder the analogous situation in two dimensions. Suppose you are trying to convince a Flatlander that a cube exists by drawing a picture of one. (Fig. 9-5, last chapter.) As the Flatlander examined your picture, his reply would likely be,

"You keep on telling me of this other world and its unimaginable shapes which you call solid. But isn't it very suspicious that all the shapes which you offer me as images or reflections of the solid ones turn out on inspection to be simply the old two-dimensional shapes of my own world as I have always known it? Is it not obvious that your vaunted other world, so far from being the archetype, is a dream which borrows all its elements from this one?"[1]

To explain a cube to a Flatlander, we simply must use two-dimensional figures. In the same way since we are physical beings, our spiritual experiences can and in fact must be described in psychological, biological, or chemical terms. But this in no way denies the existence of spiritual reality.

A more fanciful possibility is to use four dimensions to interpret the brotherhood of man. If I were to stick my five fingers on one hand into the plane of Flatland, the inhabitants of that plane would see five distinct objects, the planar cross-sections of my fingers. They would not suspect, in fact, could not be made to believe, that they were all parts of the same object. If we are three- dimensional cross-sections of four-dimensional reality, perhaps we are parts of the same body. In fact, the Bible tells us that Christians are parts of the same body in some way. This four-dimensional idea just may help us to see it more clearly. Can you imagine the five cross-sections of fingers fighting and hurting each other? That is as ridiculous as the members of the church fighting with each other. They are hurting themselves. It reminds me of the Peanut's cartoons in which the various parts of Snoopy's body are arguing with each other. This usually takes place while Snoopy is jogging. The ludicrous part is that each part of his body is talking as if it were a completely separate entity from the rest of the body. It is just as preposterous for Christians to act as if each was a separate entity. Also, we are told that in Adam all men died, in Christ all men live, and the church is one body. Perhaps we are more closely related to each other than we realize.

Our experience is that space has three dimensions and that time is linear or one-dimensional. The one dimension that time has is also special in that, in our experience, it proceeds in one direction only. We cannot travel backward in time, only forward, and we have no control over the rate of travel. It is clear from the Bible that time for God is different than time is for us. "With the Lord one day is as a thousand years and a thousand years as one day" (II Peter 3:8). Even more interesting is John 9:58: "Jesus said to them, 'Truly, truly, I say to you, before Abraham was I am.'" Notice that Jesus is not saying he was before Abraham. He uses the present tense for what would have to be past tense for us. We do not know what time is like for God, but we do know that it is different than it is for us.

C. S. Lewis has used the idea of higher dimensions in many of his books. Anyone interested in seeing other ways in which he and other writers used the concept might want to read the article, "Higher Dimensions: C. S. Lewis and Mathematics" in Volume 13 of *Seven: An Anglo-American Literary Review* published by the Marion E. Wade Center of Wheaton College. Lewis even has some interesting comments on time in several of his books. In an unfinished, but published, work of fiction entitled "The Dark Tower,"[2] he explores at some length the idea that time is two-dimensional. Maybe in heaven, time and space will be of higher dimension than we experience now. It is possible that we will move into ever higher dimensions, always "further in and higher up." All of this conjecture about dimensions is fantasy on our part. Just one thing we know: if our conjectures are wrong, the reality will be even better.

Paul tells us, "I know a man in Christ who fourteen years ago was caught up to the third heaven—whether in the body or out of the body I do not know, God knows—and he heard things that cannot be told, which man may not utter" (II Cor. 12:2-4). It is thought by some that he was referring to himself. Certainly, John's experience must have been similar. They saw things that simply do not fit our categories, perhaps our dimensions, and so are extremely difficult to explain to others. The square could have described his experiences in three dimensions in the same words Paul used. It may be that our difficulty in understanding the descriptions of beings and things in the book of Revelation is because higher dimensions are involved. At least it is interesting to read that book with the fourth or higher dimensions in mind.

In conclusion, this imaginative construct of man's mind may or may not be a part of reality, but it does help me at least "to see through a glass darkly." Its value lies not just in its own role as a model to help us understand reality, but perhaps even more important to exercise and stretch our faculty of imagination so that it might produce even better models. Before it could be helpful it had to first be imagined, then reason was used to develop it and to apply it. In man's endeavors, faith, love, and imagination are the life giving forces. In every case, reason has the less important but essential role of evaluating the options, choosing one, and activating the will.

Faith and Obedience

"Faith is obedience, not confidence."

George MacDonald

Before closing Part I - Faith and Reason, I think we should consider one more problem about the relation of faith and knowledge or
certainty. The problem for some of us has been how can we believe
something if it does not seem to us to be true? The solution of the
problem involves the question of what faith really is. Obedience has a
significant role in the solution of this problem.

We may never experience absolute certainty in this world. Still,
there is overwhelming evidence for many things. I am confident that I
am holding a pen in my hand, that I am sitting on a chair, and that there
are trees outside my window. And one more thing, I am confident that
all (or at least nearly all) reasonable people would agree with these
statements if they were here to observe my surroundings.

Why does God not give us overwhelming evidence that the Bible
is true? Surely, if God is all-powerful, he could do so. A common
answer given by many intelligent Christians (including C. S. Lewis) is
that if God would give compelling evidence, then we would not need
any faith and God wants us to have faith. I believe that there is some
truth in this answer, but that it is misleading and that a profound insight
is lost because of it.

According to this view, it seems that God is testing us. He could
convince us, but instead He chooses to leave us partly in the dark to see
if we will have faith in Him. I used to wish, fervently, that God would
show His power so clearly that I would know without any doubt that
He exists and also make clear to me His will for my life. I thought that
I wanted to believe, but how could I just make myself believe?

There were paradoxes in Christianity that made it difficult for me to
believe. I felt a little like Alice in Wonderland who said that she couldn't
believe something that was impossible even after the White Queen told
her that she only needed to try harder. After all, the queen could be-

lieve as many as six impossible things before breakfast by just trying hard. It did not seem fair to me that God did not give us more evidence.

I think that an incorrect or incomplete understanding of what faith in Jesus Christ means was at the heart of my difficulty. An incident from George Orwell's novel *1984* helped me to see more clearly into this problem. In the novel, O'Brian, on behalf of Big Brother, is trying to convince Winston that he is holding up five fingers when he is actually holding up only four. Because O'Brian punishes him painfully every time he says four, Winston finally says five. However, O'Brian is not satisfied. He knows that Winston still believes that there are only four. O'Brian wants Winston to really experience reality as Big Brother describes it to him. Winston believes that Big Brother exists and has the power to make him agree with whatever Big Brother says and yet he cannot at this point experience reality as Big Brother says it is. He does not have "faith" in Big Brother. When Winston said five, he was like the man in a story I once heard who believed that he was Napoleon. While taking a lie detector test, he was asked if he was Napoleon. Knowing that the questioner did not believe he was Napoleon and did not like to hear him make that claim, he craftily answered, "No." The lie detector indicated that he was lying!

Now, let's turn this story upside down. Suppose that Winston has become confused about reality and Big Brother is only trying to get him to see things as they really are. The power and the pain could make Winston say that there are five fingers (and now there really are five), but he only sees, or believes that he only sees, four. I believe that we are like Winston in this version of the story. Because of the Fall, we do not experience reality as it actually is. God is trying to get us to see things as they really are, to see reality through His eyes. Although, of course, God does not torture us to make us believe, it might be easy enough for Him to make us believe that He is God and that we should agree with whatever He says. However, such coercion would not ensure that we would experience that reality. We would be like Winston agreeing that there are five fingers when in fact he only sees four.

Having faith in Jesus Christ does not mean just believing that He is God. It means really believing that what He said about us is true. It means really believing that God is love, that our happiness is found in humility, and many other things that we, in our fallen state, do not experience. Many believe that Jesus is God. The devils believe that. Many even believe that the Bible is God's inerrant word, but still do not see, as God sees, that the meek are blessed and that love for and submission to others is the path to happiness. They even devise involved explanations for what Jesus "really" meant.

Faith in Jesus Christ means trusting Him, seeing the world through His eyes. This is what He is trying to do for us. A raw display of power will not lead to that kind of faith. That is why His task is so much more difficult, why He had to come to us in love and humility, suffering death on a cross to show us that love, and why in John 17 Jesus said that the way the world will know that God sent Him and that God loves us is through the loving unity His followers demonstrate.

If we could see reality as God sees it, we would know the truth about reality. This helps me understand why we have the problem, but still doesn't completely solve the problem of how to believe if it does not seem like there is enough evidence. If I don't believe, I am not like the White Queen who could just try harder and make herself believe. Kierkegaard says we must take a leap of faith. My early understanding of Kierkegaard was that we could never know by looking at the evidence whether or not Christianity was true. We are completely in the dark. We are like men, in a night with absolutely no light who come to a chasm. We can feel that he is at the edge of a drop-off. We can't feel the bottom or the other side. The chasm might be a few feet or a few hundred feet deep. It could be a few feet wide or there might not be another side. We must either leap or not. Now I would have to be pursued very closely by something extremely dangerous before I would make that kind of leap.

Since I believe that there is good evidence for Christianity and cannot believe that God would put us into that position on the chasm's edge, I could not agree with Kierkegaard. And therefore, I didn't persevere in reading his works. Then a friend of mine, Vernard Eller, who is a theologian and a student and admirer of Kierkegaard, explained to me what Kierkegaard really believed. He said that we start by not knowing if Christianity is true and, and we then must accept or reject it. This is one of those decisions we must make. If we say we will not decide, we are rejecting Christianity, not taking the leap of faith. Also, this is not a trivial issue. As C. S. Lewis has said, if Christianity is true, it is of infinite importance. Therefore, a reasonable man will look for evidence. Now according to Kierkegaard, no matter how hard one works at this, the stack of evidence for Christianity will exactly balance the stack of evidence against it. I suppose the more clever a person is, the higher the two stacks will be, but they will always be level.

Now one must decide to jump or not to jump. It would seem that half would jump and half not. However, here is where an amazing thing happens. According to Kierkegaard, everyone who honestly faces the issue and seeks the right answer will be led by the Holy Spirit to jump. Maybe this is not so amazing. After all, Jesus said, "Seek and ye shall find" (Matt. 7:7), and "If any man's will is to do His will, he shall know whether the teaching is from God" (John 7:17). Notice that one must be willing to obey.

This interpretation of the leap in the dark makes much more sense. I still don't quite agree with Kierkegaard completely. I believe that as we accumulate evidence, some will be for and some against but overall, the evidence for faith will predominate. Paul Tillich gave a definition of faith with another image:

> Faith…does not mean the belief in assertions for which there is no evidence. It never meant that in genuine religion, and it never should be abused in this sense. But faith means being grasped by a power that is greater than we are, a power which shakes us, and transforms us and heals us. Surrender to this power is faith."[1]

I like this image of a surrender better than a leap. But in any case, we have reason to believe that there is a Power who desires to grasp us and that it is the height of rationality to surrender to that Power.

Surrendering our wills to God is certainly a Biblical teaching. In science also, one must be willing to give up preconceived ideas and follow the facts wherever they lead. As E. Stanley Jones said,

This method of self-surrender is not something introduced by religion to minister to weak and fearful souls who are afraid to live. It is something inherent in the very process of knowledge, something without which we simply know nothing anywhere. Be proud and self-sufficient and unbending and the universe is a sealed book to you. Surrender yourself to the facts as a little child and everything is open to you.[2]

At first the question "Is Christianity true" appears to be a purely intellectual problem. If it were, then the most intelligent people would be more likely to get the right answer than the rest of us. However, it is the humble and the child-like who are willing to surrender their own wills to do the will of God who will know the truth. Jesus said, "Ye shall know the truth and the truth shall make you free" (John 8:32). But how shall we know the truth? John 8:32 is the last part of a sentence that begins in the 31st verse. "If ye continue in my word, then are ye my disciples indeed; and ye shall know the truth and the truth shall make you free." Here we have the conditions for knowledge. If we continue in His word and are His disciples, then we shall know. A disciple is one who follows or obeys another. So if we study His word and obey as we understand, then we will know the truth. Obedience leads to knowledge.

In Col. 1:9-10, we have another statement of the relationship between obedience and knowledge. "...we have not ceased to pray for you, asking that you may be filled with the knowledge of His will in all spiritual wisdom and understanding, to lead a life worthy of the Lord, fully pleasing to him, bearing fruit in every good work and increasing in the knowledge of God." Here we have Paul praying that the

Colossians might see reality as God sees it (as the Phillips' translation puts it). Then that knowledge will lead to obedience, "every good work". And finally it will lead back to more knowledge. Knowledge will lead to obedience and then to more knowledge.

A paradox in this obedience/knowledge cycle is pointed out and resolved in one of George MacDonald's novels by means of the following conversation between an unbelieving man and his niece.

Yes, yes! but how is one to know what is true my dear? There are so many differing claims to the quality!" exclaims the uncle. "I have been told and believe it with all my heart," replied the niece, "that the only way to know what is true is to do what is true." "But you must know what is true before you can begin to do what is true." "Everybody knows something that is true to do—that is something he ought to lose no time in setting about. The true thing is the thing that must not be let alone but done. It is much easier to know what is true to do than what is true to think. But those who do the one will come to know the other—and none else, I believe.[3]

As MacDonald says in another place, "I only pray you to obey, and assert that thus only can you fit yourself for understanding the mind of Christ." We often use the uncle's excuse that we don't even know where to start, but that is a poor excuse since we all know some things we should be doing but aren't. These things often seem like little things, such as a kind word or deed to someone near us, or reading the Bible, but they are essential things on the path to greater knowledge. In Romans 2, Paul says that we are all without excuse. We all know enough to get started. In MacDonald's words again, "The only way to learn the rules of anything practical is to begin to do the thing. We have enough knowledge in us...to begin anything required of us. The sole way to deal with the profoundest mystery...is to begin to do some duty revealed by [it] ."[4]

Jesus emphasized the importance of obedience at the close of the Sermon on the Mount when He said, "Not everyone who calls me 'Lord, Lord' will enter the kingdom of Heaven, but only those who do the will of my heavenly Father" (Matt. 7:21, NEB). Jesus went on to tell the parable of the wise man who built his house upon the rock and the foolish man who built on the sand. The wise man is one who hears Jesus' words and obeys. His house stands. The foolish man is like one who hears but does not obey. Storms and floods destroy that house. Another time, Jesus told about two sons. One says he will do what his father asks and then does not do it. The other says he won't but then does. Rhetorically, Jesus asked, "Which son did his father's will?" The answer is obvious.

E. Stanley Jones commented on the relation of obedience or action to faith or knowledge.

> In a moral universe the deepest method, the only method, of knowledge is moral response. The idea that belief is a set of intellectual conceptions apart from action is false. The word "belief" comes from 'by-lief' or 'by-life'"—the thing you live by. Your beliefs, then are the things you believe in sufficiently to act upon, to live by. The unity of theory and practice is a fact. Your theory is your practice, the only theory you have. So when we talk about surrender to the will of God, we do not talk about acquiescence to the will of God, a kind of passive acceptance of whatever comes to us—not that—but a positive bringing of everything in one's life in line with the will of God and then actively cooperating with that will as it is revealed to us in every phase of our lives.[5]

As James 2:14-26 says, faith must automatically lead to obedience. And Paul, right after he rightly says that we are saved by grace through faith and not by works, says, "We are His workmanship, created in Christ Jesus for good works, which God prepared beforehand, that we should walk in them" (Eph. 2:10, underlining mine). We will consider this matter again in later chapters, "Magic, Mirage, or Miracle" and "Knowledge, Love, and Obedience."

This chapter will close with another conversation from another MacDonald novel. This time a husband and wife are discussing faith, and the wife has described two kinds of faith. One kind, which she labels the lower faith, is intellectual belief in every fact recorded in the Bible about Jesus as Lord. The second kind of faith, which she labels the higher faith, is one that rests in the will and results in obedience. The husband then comments, "I don't at the moment see how the higher faith, as you call it, can precede the lower." To which the wife replies, "It seems to me possible enough. For what is the test of discipleship the Lord lays down? Is it not obedience? 'If ye love me, keep my commandments.' 'If a man love me, he will keep my commandments.' 'I never knew you: depart from me, ye workers of iniquity.' Suppose a man feels in himself that he must have some savior or perish; suppose he feels drawn, by conscience, by admiration, by early memories, to the form of Jesus dimly seen through the mists of ages; suppose he cannot be sure there ever was such a man, but reads about Him, and ponders over the words attributed to Him until he feels that they are the right thing whether He said them or not, and that if he could but be sure there were such a being, he would believe in Him with heart and soul; suppose also that he comes upon the words, 'If any man is willing to do the will of the Father, he shall know whether I speak of myself or He sent me;' I cannot tell whether all this is true, but I know nothing that seems half so good, and I will try to do the will of the Father in the hope of the promised knowledge.' Do you think God would or would not count that to the man for faith?"[6]

Yes, I certainly believe God would! I believe that faith is an intellectual assent to the doctrinal teaching of Christianity and a radical and total commitment to Christ as Lord of one's life, an abandonment of trust in oneself, a reliance on Christ for salvation, a reliance on the power of the Spirit for strength, and a reliance on and obedience to God. It is seeing reality as God sees it and that results in living life as God knows it must be lived. We become able to see as God sees, first by being willing to do His will and then as we see more clearly we follow Him more nearly.

Part II
Love & Logic

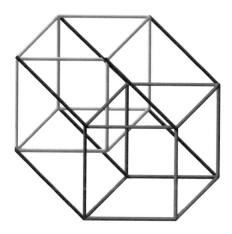

"'Narnia, Narnia, Narnia, awake. Love. Think. Speak. Be walking trees. Be divine waters.'

It was, of course, the Lion's voice...and all the beasts and birds in their different voices, low or high or thick or clear replied:

'Hail, Aslan. We hear and obey. We are awake. We love. We think. We speak. We know.'

'But please, we don't know very much yet,' said a nosey and snorty kind of voice."

From *The Magician's Nephew* by C. S. Lewis

Introduction

"Spiritual love lives in the clear light of service ordered by the truth."
Dietrich Bonhoeffer

This section explores the relationships between love and logic or reason. Love "delights in the truth" (I Cor. 13:6, NEB). It is not a soft, warm fluffy blanket that covers reality in an attempt at emotional ease and comfort at any cost, but it actually delights in the truth. Logic is a useful tool, when we understand its limitations, described in Part I, in arriving at truth. In order to discover the relationships, if there are any, between love and logic, we must have some understanding of each concept separately.

A brief consideration of logic will be sufficient for our purposes, the meaning of love will require a longer discussion. This is because love has so many meanings. As J. B. Phillips has said,

In modern parlance the word 'love' has become demoted and indeed debased to mean all sorts of things. A man can have a love for Beethoven's String Quartets and a love for chocolates with hard centers; he can love driving an open car at high speed; but when he wants to express what he feels for the One who has touched the deepest roots of his being and wants, as all lovers do, to declare himself, he can only use the same word! Whether it is due to paucity of language or mere carelessness, we find the same word used for a romantic but passing affection as for a lifetime's devotion and service.[1]

Thus we must attempt to define love, at least describe it, discuss its properties, and try to analyze it. Love is at the very heart of Christianity, so misunderstanding of the term can seriously distort the Christian message in so many ways. Only after this clarification has occurred can we discuss possible relations between love and logic and consider the question of whether it is logical to love.

Why is love at the heart of Christianity? First of all, Paul explicitly states that the greatest thing is love. He even does it in the context of comparing it with other great things such as faith, hope, knowledge, and prophecy. The rest of the New Testament, and in particular Jesus' teachings certainly agree with Paul's judgment.

But to say that love is_at the heart of Christianity may not be a strong enough statement. Love *is* the heart of Christianity. The Bible says that God is love. According to Leon Morris,

> This means more than that God is loving: it means that love is of the essence of his being. God loves—but not in an incidental or haphazard fashion. He loves because it is his nature to love, because it is his nature to give himself unceasingly in love.[2]

According to C. S. Lewis, the idea that God is love is either "nonsense, to say nothing of maudlin humbug, or else it is by far the most exciting statement about God"[3] to be found anywhere.

Emil Brunner said,

> The message that God is Love is something wholly new in the world. We perceive this if we try to apply the statement to divinities of the various religions of the world: Wotan is Love; Zeus, Jupiter, Brahma, Ahura Mazda, Vishnu, Allah is Love. All these combinations are obviously wholly impossible. Even the God of Plato, who is the principle of all Good, is not Love. Plato would have met the statement 'God is Love' with a bewildered shake of the head[4]

Brunner continues with a helpful analogy: one could give a lot of physical and chemical properties of radium, but if one omitted the fact that it is constantly radiating, then he has omitted its truly distinctive characteristic. In the same way, "if one speaks about God, stressing his holiness, his greatness, and his goodness but omitting the fact that he is constantly giving himself in love, one has omitted the thing that really matters."[5] Again according to Leon Morris, the cross is the essential starting point and the only means we have to understand what the love of God really is. It is by this that we know what love is: that Christ laid down his life for us. And we in turn are bound to lay down our lives for our brothers (I John 3:16, NEB). See also John 3:16 and I John 4:10.

> True love is not simple and soothing like a lullaby; it is demanding. To see love for what it is is to realize that selfishness is not an option. No one can persist in seeking the best for himself while he keeps before him what Christ has done on Calvary.[6]

Logic

"Loagic wad save a heap o' cursin' an' ill words."

George MacDonald

Logic is the science of drawing valid conclusions. That is, it is a method of labeling certain statements (conclusions) true on the basis of other statements (premises, axioms, or postulates) that are assumed to be true. There are rules that will tell us certain conclusions must be true if the hypotheses are true. Technically, the word _valid_ describes the argument as a whole rather than just the conclusion, but for brevity I will use the term "valid conclusion" when the conclusion follows validly from the premises and "invalid conclusion" when it does not. A conclusion is said to be valid if these rules say it must be true whenever the premises are true. A conclusion may be true or false if the premises are not true, but it must be true if the premises are true.

These rules of logic can be stated precisely and applied mechanically. Courses in symbolic logic explain in great detail how this is done, so it is not necessary to do that here. These rules agree with the intuition of most people. A good definition of a reasonable person might be one to whom the rules of logic are intuitively obvious! Of course, it should be observed that these rules are themselves assumptions. Deductive reasoning always involves assumptions. For our purposes, an informal, non-rigorous look at logic is all that is required.

The technical meaning of the word logic for a mathematician or philosopher is restricted to a study of drawing conclusions from stated premises by the formal rules of deductive reasoning. In common usage, however, the word simply means _reason or sound sense._ I will make some use of logic in its formal sense but also in the sense that logic refers broadly to reason. I suppose I should confess that I chose the word "logic" rather than the word "reason" in the title primarily for alliterative purposes.

The following is a classic example of a valid inference. The premises are the statements above the line and the conclusion below:

Socrates is a man.

All men are mortal.

∴ Socrates is mortal.

It should be emphasized that when we say that "Socrates is mortal" is a valid conclusion, we are not saying that it is true; we are only saying that if the premises are true, then it must be true. Without knowing the premises we could make no statement about its validity. For example, if the premises were "Socrates is an angel" and "All men are mortal," then the conclusion "Socrates is mortal" would be invalid. Or if the premises were "Socrates is a dog" and "All men are mortal," then the conclusion "Socrates is mortal" is invalid. That is, whether the conclusion is true or not, it does not follow from these premises.

Here is an example where the conclusion is invalid:

All squares are rectangles.

All squares are parallelograms.

∴ All rectangles are parallelograms.

Even though the conclusion is true, it is not valid because it does not follow from the given premises. The validity of a conclusion is independent of its truth or falsity. It is even independent of the truth or falsity of the premises. To say that a conclusion is valid simply means that if the premises are true, then the conclusion must be true.

It is even possible for a true conclusion to follow validly from false premises. For example:

If Nancy is President of the U.S., then Nancy is a Russian.

If Nancy is a Russian, then Nancy is a citizen of the U.S.

∴ If Nancy is President of the U.S., then Nancy is a citizen of the U.S.

The following is an example of a valid but false conclusion. For this to happen, at least one premise must be false.

Abraham Lincoln was a Hoosier.

If Abraham Lincoln was a Hoosier, then he was a short blond man.

∴ Abraham Lincoln was a short blond man.

The value of logic is that if we know our premises are true and our reasoning is valid, then we can know that our conclusion is true. Now we are ready, I hope, to look at some examples of logic that involve the word love.

> God possesses the quality of being logical.
> God possesses the quality of being loving.
> All qualities possessed by God are related to each other.
> ∴ The quality of being logical and being loving are related to each other.

The conclusion is valid. That is, if the premises are true, then the conclusion is true. "God possesses the quality of being logical" does not necessarily mean that He reasons temporally or linearly as we do. I believe that he is logical in that if we could understand Him perfectly, including His love, we would say He is beautifully logical. The statement, "I completely understand the relation between love and logic," would certainly be invalid and would be untrue. Still, for some time I have pondered about that relationship, and studied what the Bible and men have said about it and hope that what follows will be stimulating and profitable.

Here is a continuation of this example:

> We are created in the image of God.
> God possesses the quality of being logical.
> God possesses the quality of being loving.
> ∴ We have the ability to think logically and the ability to love.

This logical formulation is not complete because there could be disagreement about what is meant by being created in the image of God. However, I believe that love and quality of being logical is so essential to God's nature that no creature without these qualities could be said to be created in the image of God.

I John 4:8 says that God is love. Nowhere does the Bible say that God is logic, but John 1:1-5 refers to Jesus as the Word and says the Word was the creator of the world as well as the life and light of men. The Greek word here translated as "word" is "logos." Logos meant either word or reason in Greek. So we might translate John 1:1, "In the beginning was Reason and Reason was with God and Reason was God."

According to Greek philosophy the Logos of God was "the power which puts sense into the world, the power which makes the world an order instead of a chaos, the power which sets the world going and keeps it going in its perfect order" and was also "what gave a man reason, the power to think and the power to know."[1]

So, the word Logos, as used by John in the beginning of his gospel, would have made sense to the Greeks as reason (logic in its general sense) or the Mind of God. The word logic comes from the same root as the word logos.

The Jews were used to thinking of the word of God as the creating force. "By the word of the Lord, the heavens were made" (Psalms 33:6). So, Logos, as used by John, would make sense to the Jews as the Word. But also the Jews were familiar with passages like Proverbs 3:18 and 19 that say wisdom is the "tree of life" and where it says "The Lord by wisdom founded the earth." (See also Proverbs 8:22-30 on wisdom.) Wisdom is closely related to reason, so this would make sense to the Jews also.

William Temple has said that the Logos alike for Jew and Gentile represents the ruling fact of the universe and represents that fact as the self-expression of God. The Jew will remember that 'by the word of the Lord were the heavens made;' the Greek will think of the rational principle of which all natural laws are particular expressions. Both will agree that this Logos is the starting point of all things.[2]

I am not trying to imply that God is Logic or that God is Reason in anything like the way that God is Love, but God is reason in the sense that He possesses it. He is the source of all reason, and it is He who enables man to reason.

This chapter was meant to give a very brief introduction to logic, use it a little in thinking about love and logic, and explore, again very briefly, how reason is related to God. Now we must consider the meaning of love in the next chapter.

The Meaning of Love

"How love might be, hath been indeed, and is."

Robert Browning

In order to understand the meaning of a statement one must understand the meaning of each word in the statement. It is not possible, though, to define every word in a discussion without circular definitions as explained in Chapter 4 of Part I. Therefore, it should be no surprise that the word love may be impossible to define. I have not found any dictionary that gives an adequate definition of the New Testament concept of love. The _New Compact Bible Dictionary_ says that it can be defined only by listing its attributes.

In mathematics, undefined words, although they have no formal definition, must have the properties given by the postulates. If one premise is that the Bible is the word of God, then we might find the properties of love postulated in it.

I Cor. 13:4-7 postulates some properties of love.

Love is patient and kind; love is not jealous or boastful; it is not arrogant or rude. Love does not insist on its own way; it is not irritable or resentful; it does not rejoice at wrong, but rejoices in the right. Love bears all things, believes all things, hopes all things, endures all things.

This is not a definition of love, but it certainly helps to clarify the concept by listing some properties of love. This is similar to the situation in geometry where "line" is an undefined term but the postulates list some of the properties of a line. For example: every line is a set of points; and given any two points, there is exactly one line containing them. These postulates, and others, clarify the meaning of a line.

Another way of arriving at the meaning of a word is to give examples of it. And, the Bible does furnish us with many examples of love. If examples (and non-examples) of a word are chosen carefully, it only takes a few to make clear the meaning of most words.

Much can be learned about love by pondering its properties listed in I Cor. 13 and finding examples in the Bible and elsewhere of each of the properties. Henry Drummond's sermon, "The Greatest Thing in the World" is this kind of a study and has become a classic in Christian literature. In this sermon, Drummond says, "Love is not a thing of enthusiastic emotion. It is a rich, strong, manly, vigorous expression of the whole round Christian character—the Christ-like nature in its fullest development."[1] Note that Drummond's conclusion, based on study of the Bible, is that love is not just emotion. It is not just a strong liking.

Others have come to a similar conclusion. Paul Tillich says, "We have rejected the attempt to restrict love to its emotional element. But there is no love without emotional element, and it would be a poor analysis of love which did not take this element into consideration."[2] C. S. Lewis goes even further than Tillich by saying, "Love, in the Christian sense, does not mean an emotion. It is a state not of the feelings, but of the will."[3] Lewis goes on to say that we should not worry about whether or not we have the right emotion, but we should do what we know would be best for the other person. "Do not waste time bothering whether you 'love' your neighbor; act as if you did."[4] Admittedly, this may sound cold; however, a person may feel a strong emotion but be too weak-willed to do anything about it, while a person following Lewis' advice may not feel loving but will act in loving ways. I think most of us would prefer a friend of the latter type over the former. We may not be able to control our emotions directly, but we can obey God.

James agrees with this idea of love. "If a brother or sister is ill clad and in lack of daily food, and one of you says to them, 'Go in peace, be warmed and filled,' without giving them the things needed for the body, what does it profit?" (James 2:15-16). In other words, just being in the emotional state of desiring someone's welfare is not enough; action is necessary. John is even more explicit. "For this is the love of God, that we keep his commandments" (I John 5:3, also see I John 3:16-18). In Deuteronomy 30:1-6, Moses says that when you obey God, He will bless you, and furthermore "God will circumcise your heart and the heart of your offspring, so that you will love the Lord your God with all your heart and with all your soul, that you may live." It is important that we act, obey God's commands. But then God prepares our hearts so that emotionally and every other way ("all your heart and soul") we can love God. A similar order occurs in John 14:23. "Jesus answered him, 'If a man loves me, he will keep my word, and my Father will love him, and We will come to him and make Our home with him." We love Him by obeying Him, and then He and the Father live in our hearts. If God is in us, can our emotions not be right? "The fruit of the Spirit is love, joy, peace, patience, kindness, goodness, faithfulness, gentleness, self-control" (Gal. 5:22-23).

In one of his novels, George MacDonald ties together some of these ideas in just a few sentences.

> "Mr. Fuller was a middle-aged man, who all his conscious years had been trying to get nearer to his brethren, moved thereto by the love he bore to the Father. The more anxious he was to come near to God, the more he felt that the highroad to God lay through the forest of humanity. And he had learned that love is not a feeling to be called up at will in the heart, but the reward as the result of an active exercise of the privileges of a neighbor."[5]

Is love, then, the setting of the will to work for someone's welfare, or the acts we perform for the other person, or the feeling that God grants us when we have faithfully done the first two, or the combination of all three? Does it even matter which one it is as long as we know our part is to set our will with the faith that God will grant us the power to perform the specific acts? Also, of course, we need to cooperate with God to perform those acts of love. These questions are for you to ponder, not for me to answer. It seems to me, though, that love is the setting of the will to the extent that, with God's help, we perform loving acts.

It might be argued that sometimes we really want to do right (i.e. have the will), but we do not have the strength to act. This is really the tragedy of the normal human condition, but Christianity supplies the solution. I believe there is a fundamental principle of Christianity that when a man deliberately sets his face in the right direction (wills to do right), then God will supply the power to carry through. In this case, if we will to act lovingly even when we do not feel like it, God will supply the power. And, if we consistently act loving, God will eventually supply the emotion. E. Stanley Jones has said, "You have only to be willing; He does the rest. You supply the willingness and He supplies the power."[6] God will even help to inspire our wills. As Phil. 2:13 says, "It is God who works in you, inspiring both the will and the deed, for His chosen purpose" (NEB).

History has often shown that when one group or race ill-treats another group or race for economic reasons only, without any emotion, hatred for that ill-treated race always follows. The emotion of hatred is needed to justify the ill-treatment and leads to cycles of increased ill-treatment and increased hatred. The reverse of this vicious cycle can also happen. If we act lovingly, then we will feel more loving, which can lead to cycles of better treatment and more feelings of love. Some people argue that it is hypocritical to act loving when we don't feel loving. I think this is usually an excuse. It would be hypocritical to say we like, admire, or respect someone when we do not like, admire, or respect that person. It is not hypocritical to treat kindly someone for whom we do not feel affection.

The words "love" and "like" must be clearly differentiated or this whole discussion will be confusing. Many people think that "to love" means "to like an awful lot." This is illustrated by a little boy's conversation with his mother.

"I love cookies."

"No, son. You can't love cookies. You like them."

"Okay, Mom. I like cookies…but it sounds as though I'm talking about crackers."

To "like" means to feel attracted to, to enjoy, or to admire. On the other hand, love is an unselfish concern that freely accepts another in loyalty and seeks his good, according to *Webster's Seventh New Collegiate Dictionary*. Love, as I am using the term, is the commitment to personally work and sacrifice for the welfare of the object of that love. It has been said that love is "a profound concern for the welfare of another without any desire to control that other, to be thanked by that other, or to enjoy the process."[7] Thomas Merton has said that "love implies an efficacious will not only to do good to others exteriorly but also to find some good in them to which we can respond."[8] Another definition that has been given is, "Love is a well-reasoned concern for the good of all."[9] I don't think that any of these descriptions of love are adequate as a complete definition, but they do help to clarify the meaning.

Understanding the difference between "love" and "like" should keep us from the fallacy that just because we cannot like someone then we can't love him. It is possible to love someone without liking him. Sometimes I like myself, sometimes I don't. However, I almost always love myself in the sense of desiring the best for myself. Understanding the difference between "love" and "like" helps considerably in understanding the meaning of the command to "love your neighbor as yourself." This is not a command to like oneself or a command that we must have a good self-image. It first acknowledges the fact that normal people are concerned about their own welfare and then commands us to have the same concern about the welfare of others.

"Love the sinner, hate the sin" is possible. It is not just a hypocritical or self-righteous statement, and it is far from splitting hairs. I hate my own sin even though I love the sinner. It is because I love myself that I hate my sin. In fact, the more I love the sinner the more I will hate the sin.

Liking or admiring someone sometimes makes it easier for us to love him. But far from being a necessary condition, it may even hinder us in loving. Liking a child too much might lead us to avoid punishing the child when true love would demand punishment. Or, admiring a friend too much might cause us to neglect confronting him with a certain fault, when true love would demand a confrontation for the friend's welfare, not for our own. Likewise, liking one person may cause us to act unlovingly to another person and liking one group or race could lead to racism or extreme nationalism.

Moses provides us with a good example of love as the commitment to personally work and sacrifice for the welfare of the object of that love. He certainly was committed to and worked hard for the welfare of the Israelites. He also sacrificed much to lead them out of slavery into the promised land. The incident that shows the depth of Moses' sacrificial love is when he was willing to be blotted out of God's book for the sake of the sinning Israelites even though their idolatry had just caused his anger to "burn hot" (Ex. 32:19 and 32). Another time God was going to destroy the Israelites and make of Moses "a nation greater and mightier than they," but through Moses' intercession for them, the Israelites were saved (Num. 14:12-20).

Without an understanding of what love is, we would be as bewildered as most of the Washington press corps was by the following segment of a press conference they had with Mother Teresa.

"What do you hope to accomplish here?" someone shouted.

"The joy of loving and being loved," she smiled, her eyes sparkling in the face of camera lights.

"That takes a lot of money doesn't it?" another reporter threw out the obvious question. Everything in Washington costs money; and the more it costs, the more important it is.

Mother Teresa shook her head, "No, it takes a lot of sacrifice."[10]

Another example of how a better understanding of love can help us comes from the area of marriage and divorce. If people would realize before marriage that love involves commitment and sacrifice, it would solve most of the problems that lead to divorce. In fact, if each partner in a marriage were sacrificially committed to promoting the welfare of the other, there would be no need for divorce at all. What causes so many divorces is the belief that love is an emotion and therefore when the emotion ebbs for a while, the marriage should end. As Richie told his sister on the old TV comedy "Happy Days," "Love is more than queasiness." Sometimes it is the love of friends that help a couple through a difficult time. In one church, the couples in a young married fellowship helped reconcile a divorced couple. They were committed enough to go to them and say, "You can't split up, you are a part of us," and were willing to sacrifice to help them work through their problems. It is important to understand the difference between love and mere emotion.

Analyses of Love

"He grew more and more in love with Lucy. He almost loved her."

George MacDonald

C. S. Lewis divides love into three kinds: need-love, gift-love, and appreciative love.[1] An example of need-love would be a frightened child running to his mother. An example of gift-love would be a man working, saving, and planning for the future well-being of his family even though he is aware that he will not live to see the results of his hard labor. Appreciative-love could be illustrated by my study of Abraham Lincoln or watching Larry Bird play basketball.

It should be admitted that these loves overlap. The frightened child appreciates his mother and even supplies a mother's need in the act of running to her. A man may be supplying his own need to build a certain self-image by working for his family, or he may even be demanding something from his family in return. Appreciative-love, when expressed, may be a gift-love. It may also satisfy a need to look beyond one's self or a need for identification with a hero. Lewis himself says, "We murder to dissect. In actual life, thank God, the three elements of love mix and succeed one another, moment by moment. Perhaps none of them except need-love ever exists alone, in 'chemical' purity, for more than a few seconds."[2] In spite of this overlapping, the attempt to analyze is helpful. I doubt if concepts are ever pure, at least to our finite minds. One thing slides into another. Yet analysis is very useful in clarifying concepts, especially if we understand its limitations.

Need-love is the least attractive of these loves. But as fallen creatures, we need God and we need each other. There is an interesting story about a man who visited both heaven and hell. In hell, people were seated at a banquet table filled with delicious food, but the spoons had such long handles and were strapped to their arms in such a way that they could not feed themselves. Needless to say there was great agony and complaining in the group. In heaven, he saw the same situation but with no complaining. Each person was feeding the person sitting on the opposite side of the table. For some reason, God has implanted into us a need for other people as well as a need for Him. Through need-love we may approach nearer to God than any other way. Paradoxically, we may be most like God through gift-love but at the same time, because of pride, be farthest from Him. Through appreciative-love we praise God, and at the same time, satisfy our own need.

Is it possible that we can have a gift-love toward God? I think it is. For some reason, probably beyond our comprehension, He has a need that can only be satisfied by our giving of ourselves to Him. Although how He has that need I cannot comprehend, I know that He desires us to give ourselves to Him because it is the only way for us to find true happiness. Also, by giving to others, we give to Him. "And the King will answer them, 'Truly, I say to you, as you did it to one of the least of these my brethren, you did it to me'" (Matt. 25:40).

Dividing love into the three components, need-love, gift-love, and appreciative love, is not the only way of analyzing love. In *The Four Loves*, Lewis gives us another analysis by discussing four types of love: storge or affection, philia or friendship, eros or romantic love, and agape or the charity of I Cor. 13. The four loves may exist in combination. In a good marriage, the partners are not only in love but are friends and have affection for each other. In a good Christian marriage, agape, the love of I Cor. 13, is present also. It may be wondered whether logical analysis is worthwhile, or even possible, if these loves exist in shifting combinations. I think it is, because the kinds can be mentally separated and investigated, thus leading to increased understanding of the various combinations.

Storge is best illustrated by the love of parents to offspring or offspring to parents. Familiarity is essential for this love. Appreciative-love may or may not be a part of it. You might not appreciate a certain relative, life-long neighbor, or old acquaintance but still feel affection for him. Of course, affection may consist of any combination of need-love, gift-love, and appreciative-love. Affection is the most humble and least discriminating of the loves. A child may have this kind of love for a cruel, ill-mannered parent and not for a kind and decent neighbor. One perversion of need-love affection is jealousy, which may occur in a family or group when one of its members goes beyond its usual familiar patterns; for example if in a non-college educated family, one goes to college, or in a college educated family, one does not go to college. Likewise, gift-love affection is commonly perverted by putting unreasonable demands on the recipient while, at the same time, not admitting that demands are being made. It can become very selfish. C. S. Lewis illustrated this in the following poem, an epitaph on a tombstone:

Erected by her sorrowing brothers
In memory of Martha Clay.
Here lies one who lived for others;
Now she has peace, and so have they.[3]

Another aspect of true love is that if we really desire the best for another, we won't care if that best is supplied by someone other than ourselves. In one of George MacDonald's novels, a grandfather prays that he and his wife may know what to do or say that might help their wayward granddaughter. However, he ends the prayer with these words, God will "maybe let us see something we should do, or maybe do the necessary thing without using us."[4]

In another MacDonald novel, storge or affection between two sisters is described, its limitations clearly pointed out, and its possibility as a stepping stone to a better love.

The sisters were about as good friends as such negative creatures could be; and they would be such friends all their lives, if on the one hand neither of them grew to anything better, and on the other no jealousy, or marked difference of social position through marriage, intervened. They loved each other, if not tenderly, yet with the genuineness of healthy family-habit—a thing not to be despised, for it keeps the door open for something better. In itself it is not at all to be reckoned upon, for habit is but the merest shadow of reality. Still it is not a small thing, as families go, if sisters and brothers do not dislike each other.[5]

Philia, or friendship, is ignored as a love by the modern world. It is often suspected of being homosexuality. Two or more people are friends because they are interested in the same ideas or participate in the same activities. Of course, affection may and probably will enter in, but a person may have more affection for a father at the same time that he prefers discussing philately with a fellow stamp collector than being with his father.

The love David and Jonathan had for each other is a good illustration of philia. In David's lament over the death of Jonathan, he said, "I am distressed for you, my brother Jonathan; very pleasant have you been to me; your love was wonderful, passing the love of women" (II Sam. 1:26). The story of David and Jonathan shows philia at its best, producing warmth of affection, unselfishness, helpfulness, and loyalty. They probably had many common interests on which to base philia. They were both brave soldiers, patriotic Israelites, and worshipers of Jehovah.

Philia is probably the most obviously rational of the loves. It is easier to see logically why friends act as they do than lovers or people following I Cor. 13. However, later in this chapter I hope to show that even agape is logical or reasonable. As with all natural loves, philia can be good or bad. It may produce humility within a group of friends because of the respect and admiration one has for others in the group. On the other hand, it may produce pride by believing that "our group" is better than anyone outside it. In addition, friends reinforce our opinions and values, which may be good or bad depending on the opinions and values.

Most people know what is meant by eros or being "in love." One non-definition (anti-definition?) is that it is the feeling you feel when you feel the feeling you've never felt before. Eros should not be confused with lust. Lust is simply a strong desire for the physical pleasure that accompanies the sexual act. Eros means to be in love with the whole person which includes but is not restricted to sexuality. Sexuality is a part of "being in love," but when it is over-emphasized it tends to take over and then degenerates into all kinds of perversions. One problem with eros is that it may change into lust. Another is that lovers may become very exclusive and selfish because of the power of eros. But it can be beautiful also.

There are two main characteristics of eros. One is that the beloved is seen, or believed to be worthy of love. In fact, this may not be the case. Eros is the type of love for which the statement "love is blind" is sometimes true. The second characteristic is the desire to possess. Lyrics from a song that was popular several decades ago expresses this point: "I want to gain complete control of you...handle even the heart and soul of you." This shows that not all bad lyrics come from contemporary popular music! Agape is in contrast to eros on both of these points. Agape loves the unlovable and can love without possession.

Storge, philia, and eros are natural loves as contrasted with agape or Godly love. The three natural loves are neither good nor evil in themselves. Each has, at times, led people astray, but each at other times has led people aright.

There is always the temptation to depend on the natural loves, but by themselves they are not dependable. Each can be used by God as an environment in which agape can grow. Each can be used as a model of what love should be. Tolstoy says, "Love for our children, our spouse, our brothers, is a sample of the love we should and must feel for all."[6] Even eros, perhaps the most dangerous, probably gives the best taste on a strictly natural level of what pure unselfishness is. Eros makes strong promises, "I will ever be true." It recognizes what should be but cannot by itself give the power to accomplish it. Physicists use two models, waves and particles, for light. Each contributes to our understanding of light. Neither by itself is sufficient. In a similar way, storge, philia, and eros, as models of agape, contribute to our understanding of love, but none, alone, is sufficient. These three loves seem to be built into the trinity. The Christian looks to God as Father (storge), God as Bridegroom or Lover (eros), and God as Friend (philia).

Agape is the love whose properties are postulated in I Cor. 13. It is the love God has for us and the love He expects us to have for Him and for all mankind. Without God, agape is impossible. "We love, because He first loved us" (I John 4:19). Because we were created in the image of God, we have the ability to love. But it has been impaired by the Fall. I think that everyone has this gift of God, the ability to love, in some measure. Some seem to have it much more than others, some non-Christians more than some Christians. The real difference between Christians and non-Christians is that the true Christian has contact with God, the source of love, and hence his ability, to love being nourished and strengthened, is a growing thing.

The Greeks did not use the word agape as much as eros or philia. It was used at times as a synonym or stylistic variation for the other terms for love. In contrast to the others, its meaning was vague, suggesting sympathy, a hospitable spirit, or general good will. The New Testament writers chose this rather bland term but infused it with the concept of love taught and exemplified by Christ. It was really a providential situation. Agape had the right general connotations, but was not a commonly used term with meanings that might confuse people when it was used for the Christian idea of love. It could be used as an undefined word in mathematics is used, with its meaning firmly established by listing its properties and by giving examples.

The New Testament does not use the word eros even though, in addition to its meanings of sexual desire, sensual longing, and passionate aspiration, Greek philosophers used it for the "upward longing to the eternal or divine." Eros, in whatever sense it was used, always included high passion, an overpowering emotion. However, although God will use emotion to appeal to us, He will not use it to overpower our wills.[7]

Lewis, contrasting eros and agape, says, "love as distinct from 'being in love' is not merely a feeling. It is a deep unity maintained by the will and deliberately strengthened by habit; reinforced by (in Christian marriages) the grace which both parents ask, and receive from God. They can have love for each other even at those moments when they do not like each other; as you love yourself even when you do not like yourself.[8]

Some people want to reject natural loves because they are rivals to agape. Some reject them because they may lead to pain. Neither are valid reasons. Anything in this world may become a rival to God and may lead to pain. The natural loves accepted for what they are can enrich our lives and teach us about agape. The better we understand them, the better we are enabled to understand agape. We should not reject natural loves, but should offer them to God. It is impossible to love (with agape love) any human too much. It is possible to love a human too much in proportion to our love of God. That is, we may love God too little rather than man too much.

Tolstoy gives another analysis by saying that there are three kinds of love, beautiful love, self-denying love, and active love. As he describes them, I would not call the first two real loves. Beautiful love is a caricature of eros and Self-denying love is a caricature of agape. Beautiful love is a love for the beauty of the sentiment of love. That is a kind of love of love itself. He does not restrict it to romantic love, but it only exists as it makes one feel good. He says that some "who love beautifully, not only tell everybody of their love, but always tell it in French...[and that love] would vanish at once were they forbidden to talk about it in French."[9]

"Self-denying love—is love of the process of sacrificing oneself for the beloved object regardless of whether such sacrifice benefits or harms the loved one."[10] This parody of agape would do anything "for the beloved" provided only the whole world knows what a wonderful love I am capable of and regardless of whether it benefits the beloved! Active love, as he describes it, is very like true agape in that one is willing to do whatever really benefits the object of the love. I believe that most of us fall into the first two classifications more than we would like to admit.

One may wonder whether all this analysis of love is useful or helpful in any way. As mentioned earlier, it is my belief that a better understanding of love will be helpful in many ways in our relation with God and man. And it is my hope that this discussion has led to a better understanding. Perhaps it would be good to look at some applications. I have already mentioned some. For example, to love our neighbor as ourselves does not mean trying to work up a warm emotion or an admiration for the neighbor; it does mean being as concerned about our neighbor's welfare as our own and as willing to work for it as for our own.

A good understanding of love is necessary to understand Matt. 6:24. "No one can serve two masters for either he will hate the one and love the other, or he will be devoted to one and despise the other. You cannot serve God and mammon." I often wondered why it should be impossible for me to like or admire two different masters. Please note that we are dealing with masters not with just any two people. It is possible to like each of two masters. What is impossible is to serve two masters. If there are really two, then there will be a difference sometime in their wills. At that point, I would have to choose which to obey. My will would have to go along with one not both. I could still have a feeling of affection for each. What is required by masters is obedience, and so my love in the sense of obedience would have to go with just one of the masters. There is a similar situation in Luke 14:26-27. "If any one comes to me and does not hate his own father and mother and wife and children and brothers and sisters, yes, and even his own life, he cannot be my disciple. Whoever does not bear his own cross and come after me, cannot be my disciple." I don't think that this means we should have the emotion of hatred against these people, but our wills must go against theirs every time their wills are against God's will. Again, it is a question of the will and obedience rather than the emotions.

An incorrect understanding of love leads to problems with statements like "For the Lord disciplines him whom he loves, and chastises every son whom he receives" (Heb. 12:6). Many parents believe that they cannot punish their children because they love them too much. In every human life, both as child and adult, there are times when discipline, chastisement, and punishment are essential for that person's welfare. At those times, the logic of love must overcome the weakness of emotion and be tough, strong, and gentle. Paul often shows this willingness to be strong, even to seem harsh, rather than wishy-washy in his epistles. For example, in I Cor. 4:14 he says, "I do not write this to make you ashamed, but to admonish you as beloved children." He loves them as his own children even though he follows this admonition with some frank statements in Chapter 5. He also uses very strong language in Galatians, Chapter 4. He loves them enough to cause them some minor and temporary pain in order to produce a major and permanent good. This is only logical.

The Best Love, Logic

"Feeling is far from sufficient."
Elton Trueblood

The lyrics of a popular song proclaim, "What the world needs now is love sweet love. It's the only thing that there's just too little of." According to my oldest daughter, my first reaction to those words was, "A little more brainpower wouldn't hurt anything either." Whether or not love is the only thing there is too little of depends, of course, on the meaning and object of love. We are even told that a certain kind of love is the root of all evil. "For the love of money is the root of all evil" (I Tim. 6:10). Philia is the Greek word here translated as love. This verse shows the importance of the object of love. Furthermore, if only emotion is meant by love, it certainly is not enough. "Affection produces happiness if - and only if - there is common sense and give and take and decency.... The mere feeling is not enough. You need 'common sense,' that is reason."[1]

We have all known people whose "heart is in the right place" but who, through thoughtlessness, often hurt others. In fact, we probably all fit in that category too often. A friend confessed in a recent Sunday morning sermon, "Possibly, my number one sin is thoughtlessness." We may have the correct emotional desire for someone's welfare and still do things against that welfare.

Elton Trueblood has summarized this thought so well and even stated it in logical terms.

We know something when we know that, whatever the problem, we must always be loving. We do not know, in our finitude, which of various possible pathways is the really loving one, but the effort to discover it is an immense help. While the demand of love in always the major premise, we must use our common sense and reason and experience to know what the minor premise may be. I know I must be loving to the beggar who approaches me, but only reason can help me to know whether it is more loving to give him money or to withhold it and to help in some other way. In short, the recognition of the Christian absolute, while it gives us a firm base in principle, does not relieve us of the necessity of hard thinking.[2]

In trying to decide what we should do to help the beggar mentioned in the last paragraph, it is important to be able to reason so that we can do what is best for him. Our minds can be used to rationalize as well as to reason. The more ability one has to reason, the better one can rationalize also. To rationalize means to find reasons or excuses for whatever it is that we desire. In this example, we might desire, perhaps subconsciously, to do nothing and so we find "reasons" for doing exactly that, nothing. On the other hand we may desire not to "get involved" so we find excuses to give him a little money so we can feel good and then forget about it.

There is a lady in one of George MacDonald's novels who has great compassion for all who are suffering from injustice. She is always rushing into situations and trying to set things right with her money, of which she has a great deal. However, she does not think and so she does not use her money wisely and does not understand that suffering may have good results. As a result, she often accomplished nothing or more evil than good. MacDonald says,

> She could have taken the whole world to her infinite heart, and in unwisdom coddled it into corruption. Praised be the grandeur of the God who can endure to make and see His children suffer. Thanks be to Him for His north winds and His poverty, and His bitterness that falls upon the spirit that errs: let those who know Him, thus praise the Lord for His goodness.[3]

Later she is helped to begin to think more clearly and to use reason in helping others. Through reason and the Spirit's guidance, money can be used to help others, but as Mother Teresa has said, sacrifice is more important than money.

Love, as a desire to help the people in strife-torn situations such as in Ireland, Israel, Africa, and Eastern Europe, is necessary but not sufficient. Much time, thought, dedication, and tough-minded study, not by individuals, but by cooperating groups of people, must go into the search for solutions. And prayer for God's help is essential.

It is probably more important in today's society than ever before to be able to combine logic with love. The principle illustrated by the parable of the Good Samaritan is that we should help anyone who is in need whom we can be aware of, and whom we are in a position to help. Because of the nature of communication and transportation today, we are aware of and could help many people. The needs are tremendous. Most of us in America could help, if we would. None of us, alone, would be able to satisfy the needs of everyone in the world. Each of us must decide how we can do the most good and for whom, when, and where. To do this we need all the help reason can give us. We might have the right feelings and the best intentions and be not only ineffective but, in the complex situations in our world, might actually be harmful to those we are trying to help. It is so complicated that many give up and say, "There is nothing we can do." Sometimes this is just another example of rationalization, but it is difficult to know what to do.

Since God is all-powerful and loving, it is only reasonable to ask Him to guide us in these difficult situations and in all of our relationships with others. In the last year of his life, Leo Tolstoy records the following in what was meant to be his private diary.

I am used to praying when I am alone, thank God. But when I come together with other people, I need more than ever to pray, I still cannot get used to it. I shall try with all my strength to teach myself when I meet or deal with anyone always to say to myself: "Help me, Lord, to treat him or her with brotherly love."

I do believe that God will help us if we ask for help and are using the resources we have, but we must remember that our minds and the capability of developing them are part of the resources God has already given us. God expects us to use our minds to think as well as our hands to work and our tongues to pray.

"You shall love the Lord your God with all your hearts, and with all your soul, and with all your mind, and with all your strength" (Mark 12:30). This verse certainly implies that we should use our minds. It is possible though to use this verse to rationalize. For example, we might desire to have a beautiful air-conditioned church with padded pews and the finest organ money can buy, so we use this verse, which calls on us to love God with everything we have, to justify having that kind of a church building. After all, we say, our church should be at least as nice as our homes. But if we are really reasoning instead of just rationalizing, we would know that the next verse after Mark 12:30 says, "You shall love your neighbor as yourself," and then maybe our homes and cars ought not to be so luxurious when there are people in so much need. Perhaps we can best express our love to God with a simpler lifestyle and worship in a plainer building so that we can help those people in need. Abraham Lincoln was a good example of combining love and logic. An acquaintance of his once wrote, "Mr. Lincoln was not a man of strong attachments—he was the friend of few men but he was the true friend of Mankind. He loved man as he loved God, logically."[4] Lincoln's emotions were not always apparent, but he did what he could to help others. As a politician he used his mind to do the good that he could do and did not waste time and energy trying to do something that was impossible.

In the area of romantic love, also, thoughtfulness is important. Perhaps people are hurt more because of thoughtlessness in this relationship than in any other. MacDonald shows what eros should be when he describes one of his characters as follows,

> He loved as a man loves who has thought seriously, specu-
> lated, tried to understand; whose love therefore is consistent
> with itself, harmonious with its nature and history, changing
> only in form and growth, never in substance and character…
> The painter was not merely in love with Florimel: he loved
> her.[5]

The best way to love, in fact, the only effective way, is to be thoughtful, to be logical. If we sincerely desire someone's welfare and if we know what will produce that welfare, then we will do it. Thought is required to find what will produce that welfare. If I wanted to oversimplify so that we could produce a motto on a bumper sticker (The only bumper sticker I was ever tempted to buy said, "Down With Bumper Stickers"), it would say "Logic is the best love."

Lewis gives us a good illustration of this relation between love and logic with the garden and the gardener. A garden is beautiful because of two things: nature and a gardener. Without the gardener, there is no garden, only a wilderness. Without nature, there is no garden, in fact, nothing. Therefore, nature is much more important than the gardener. Nature supplies the life-giving part. A wilderness may be beautiful, but it is not a garden. The gardener is necessary to trim some parts, cut out certain things altogether, and cultivate others. Similarly, a good relationship is beautiful because of love and logic. Both are essential, but love is more important than logic. Love supplies the life-giving power. However, logic is as necessary to the relationship as the gardener is to the garden. Logic must trim some parts, cut out certain things altogether, and cultivate others.

The Best Logic, Love

"O God, who art the truth, make me one with Thee in everlasting love."

Thomas a Kempis

In the last chapter we saw that the best way to love is to be logical, which may not be too profound once one ponders it. However, although it may seem strange, in many situations it is also true that the best logic is love. Logic is used to prove things. In this chapter we will consider how love is the logic that proves Christianity is true. That is, in the proof for Christianity, "the best logic is love."

I believe that Christianity is a reasonable religion. As a model for reality, it contains paradoxes for our finite minds, but in comparison with all other conceivable models, it best fits the facts. In reasoning with unbelievers we may appeal to the existence of moral law, the truth of the Biblical statements that can be verified, historical evidence of Biblical events, personal experience and the personal experience of other Christians, scientific evidence, and the weakness of alternative (i.e. non-Christian) models. All of these may be useful in convincing someone of the truth of Christianity, but Jesus has given us one reason that is sure to convince.

John 17 contains the longest recorded prayer of Jesus. It occurred on the night before His crucifixion. In it He says, "I do not pray for these only, but also for those who are to believe in Me through their word" (John 17:20). That is, He is praying for His disciples and for all Christians, because anyone who is a Christian today has come to believe because of the word of those disciples. He is praying for all Christians, "that all of them may be one, Father, just as you are in me and I am in you. May they also be in us so that the world may believe that you have sent me" (John 17:21). Of all things Jesus might have asked His Father to give us, power to heal the sick or perform other miracles, great eloquence to preach the gospel, or other conspicuous powers, He only asked that we have the same kind of unity that the Father and Son have. Now this unity is certainly based on love. Probably, there is no true unity that is not based on love. And one result of this loving unity is that people will know that Jesus was sent from God.

This idea is so important that Jesus repeats and expands it in verses 22 and 23. "I have given them the glory that you gave me, that they may be one as we are one: I in them and you in me. May they be brought to complete unity to let the world know that you sent me and have loved them even as you have loved me." He concludes this prayer in verse 26 by asking "that the love you have for me may be in them and that I myself may be in them." So Jesus is saying that if we love each other as the Father and Son love each other then the world will know that Jesus was sent from God and that God loves them.

Here we have the best proof, the absolutely convincing proof that Jesus was sent from God and that God loves the world. On the authority of Jesus himself, if we as Christians have the same loving unity or oneness that the Father and Son have, then the world <u>will know</u>. It is that love in you and me that binds us together and manifests itself to the people of the world in ways that they will know that there is something supernatural in our unity and will see that Jesus is from God and that God loves them. So "they will know that we are Christians by our love" and not only know we are Christians, but also know that Christianity is true.

So this is the best of proofs. People see the love that is in the body of believers and come to believe themselves. In Acts 2:44-47 we read, "And all that believed were together, and had all things common; And sold their possessions and goods, and parted them to all men, as every man had need. And they, continuing daily with one accord in the temple, and breaking bread from house to house, did eat their meat with gladness and singleness of heart, Praising God, and having favour with all the people. And the Lord added to the church daily such as should be saved." (KJV). This is a beautiful picture of loving community leading to the saving of souls. In later church history also we hear of non-Christians looking on and saying, "Behold how they love one another."

What has happened to the church? It is still true that in many cases people are coming to believe because of the love they see in the body of Christ, yet too often we hear people say, "If that's the way Christians treat each other, then I want nothing to do with it." Paul paints the picture quite clearly in II Cor. 12:20 when he says to the Corinthian Church that he is afraid he will find in them, "strife, jealousy, angry tempers, disputes, slanders, gossip, arrogance, disturbances." This best of proofs, then, has become the worst of proofs. Instead of unbelievers looking at the church, seeing unity, and proof that Christianity is true, they too often see disunity, and what seems to them proof that Christianity is false.

This strife within the church, which turns the best proof into the worst proof is due primarily to our self-centeredness, our lack of humility. It is a concern for my rights that leads me to strife with you and keeps God's love from flowing through me to you. I believe that there is an overemphasis today, even within evangelical Christianity, on self-love. We need to realize that we are important, because God made us in His image and Christ died for us. But that should lead us to realize that every human being was created in the image of God and Jesus died for each one. Furthermore, it should take our minds off of ourselves and make us think first about God and then about our fellow creatures. In order to have the humility we need to properly love each other, we really need a vision of God and a vision of our fellow man. This matter of humility is so important that we will devote a later chapter to it.

When the church is this loving community, the love does not stay within the group. It spills over in specific acts of love for all those who are in contact with it. Many people who would say they are unbelievers because of purely intellectual problems are won by these acts of love. Madeleine L'Engle's experience, which she related in *A Circle of Quiet* is a good illustration of this. She had talked to many minister friends about her intellectual doubts, and they recommended all kinds of theological books that were of no help. Then she talked to Canon Tallis who listened to her intellectual arguments in silence as though he knew they were not the important thing. In her own words,

Tallis who listened to her intellectual arguments in silence as though he knew they were not the important thing. In her own words,

> Then something happened, something so wounding that it cannot possibly be written down. Think of two of the people you love most in the world; think of a situation in which both are agonizingly hurt and you are powerless to do anything to help. It is far easier to bear pain for ourselves than for those we love, especially when part of it is that we cannot share the but pain must stand by, unable to alleviate it.
>
> Canon Tallis hardly knew us at all, then. But he stepped in. What he did is involved with all that I cannot write. The point right now is that this was the moment of light for me, because it was an act of love, love made visible.
>
> And that did it. Possibly nothing he could have done for me, myself, would have illuminated the world for me as did this act of love towards those I love. Because of this love, this particular (never general) Christian love, my intellectual reservations no longer made the least difference. I had seen love in action, and that was all the proof I needed.[1]

So, if we really want to prove that Christianity is true, then the most logical thing to do is to love. It is really true that in this case, the best logic is love.

Humility

"Love—which means humility"
Thomas Merton

Without doubt, the New Testament teaches that agape love is the greatest Christian virtue. Also, the Bible seems to teach that pride is the greatest sin. It was the sin which caused Satan to be cast out of heaven and the sin that caused Eve to disobey God. In *Mere Christianity*, C. S. Lewis has a chapter on pride which he entitles "The Great Sin." This is a chapter that every Christian should read. Actually, I think that everyone should read the whole book. In that chapter he says, "According to Christian teachers, the essential vice, the utmost evil, is Pride... Pride leads to every other vice: it is the complete anti-God state of mind."[1]

Here is a paradox. If pride is the greatest vice, then its opposite, humility, should be the greatest virtue. On the other hand, if love is the greatest virtue, then its opposite should be the greatest vice. But what is the opposite of agape love? Perhaps it is love of self, that is, pride. And Thomas Merton equates love with humility. That would resolve the paradox. However, it doesn't completely satisfy me.

Humility and love are very closely related. Without humility it would be impossible to love. Pride would interfere with my dedication to promote your welfare. Still, there does seem to be some difference between humility and love. We may be getting into trouble again because of our Western culture's predilection to analyze everything. It may be that there is only one Christian virtue, which is His righteousness, godliness, or Christ-likeness. If so, then every virtue is only a facet of that one. Love and humility are just aspects of Christ-likeness. I think this is closer to the truth. Under this view, love is still the most important facet but humility is very close to love. And as I said before, analysis can still be useful as long as we understand its limitations.

Humility is usually defined as lack of pride and pride is defined as an overly high opinion of oneself. Humility is having a correct opinion of oneself, not, as some believe, having a low opinion of oneself. We might even say it is to see ourselves as God sees us. Love must start with that, but must also include seeing others as God sees them.

Humility comes from the same root as humus, that is, soil. We must know that we are not God, but are earthly. Meekness is a synonym for humility. And related to the word meek is muck. Muck is rich soil or even moist manure. Again, a reminder of our lowly status. But also, humility is a condition conducive to healthy growth. I hope this word study is not too earthy for you. I like it, and I think it is apt.

Self-centeredness is not the same as pride, but is closely related to it. A person may be self-centered, that is, may think of himself constantly without thinking highly of himself. But constantly thinking of ourselves even if it is thinking ill of ourselves, keeps us from loving others. Somehow, I must get my attention away from myself.

In C. S. Lewis' fantasy, *The Great Divorce*, Ghosts (i.e. people in hell) may visit the outskirts of heaven where Spirits (i.e. people from heaven) invite them to come into heaven. They almost always refuse, and they refuse because of pride or self-centeredness. In one instance, a Spirit is trying to get one of the Ghosts to enter heaven. "'Friend' said the Spirit, 'Could you, only for a moment, fix your mind on something not yourself?' 'I've already given you my answer," said the Ghost, coldly but still tearful. 'Then only one expedient remains,' said the Spirit."[2]

At that point the Spirit blows a horn, calling a herd of gigantic unicorns. The herd thunders down on them, frightening the Ghost. The narrator who was watching is frightened also and runs away, so he does not know what happened. Later he has a chance to ask another Spirit about it and gets the following answer. "It will maybe have succeeded, ... Ye will have divined that he meant to frighten her; not that fear itself could make her less a Ghost, but if it took her mind a moment off herself, there might, in that moment, be a chance. I have seen them saved so."[3] This fictitious incident illustrates the importance of getting our minds off of ourselves. Incidentally, the book is not meant to make the claim that a choice is possible after death, only to give some insight into the nature of the choice itself. Later, we will return to this question of how to become humble. First, we will consider a Biblical example to learn more about what humility means.

Numbers 12:3 says, "Now the man Moses was very humble, more than any man who was on the face of the earth." By looking at Moses' life we ought to be able to learn something about meekness. One of the first things we know about him is that he killed an Egyptian and then ran away. No meekness evident here. So his humility must have come later. It is also not evident at the time God called him to his special task. He tried to refuse the call with the excuse that he was not qualified for it. Now this lowly opinion of himself may seem to some to be humility, but it is not. He is thinking too much about himself. If he hadn't had his mind on himself, he could have heard God telling him that He would work through him, enabling him to accomplish the release of the Hebrew slaves. Also, he could have been thinking clearly, seeing that if God was asking him to do it, then it must be possible.

It is actually in an incident where Moses appears to be anything but humble, that we can see what humility is. In Exodus 32, we are told that the Israelites made and worshiped a golden calf while Moses was on the mountain communing with God. At this point God tells Moses that he is going to destroy the people because of their sin and make a great nation out of Moses' descendants. Moses argues with God, giving Him reasons why He should not do this. "And the Lord repented of the evil which he thought to do to his people." (Ex. 32:14, KJV). Isn't this amazing arrogance on Moses' part to argue with God? No, I believe that if Moses had once thought about himself during this time, he could not have done it. It was precisely because he was thinking about the people and about God, and not about himself, that he could talk to God that way. A similar incident occurs in Numbers 14:10-20.

The importance of meekness is illustrated by an episode in Moses' life when he failed to be meek. One of the things that puzzled me for a long time was God's punishment of Moses in the matter of getting water out of a rock. Moses had accomplished it once in the correct fashion. Then, at a later time, he does it again and something goes wrong. God tells him that he will not be allowed to enter the Promised Land. Now it used to seem to me that this was very harsh on God's part. After all Moses was still so much better than the rest of the people. I had heard that it was because Moses struck the rock when God told him to speak to it and so it was disobedience that brought about the severe punishment. However, in the passage (Numbers 20:1-13) God tells him to speak to the rock and says nothing at all about striking or not striking the rock. On the previous occasion, Moses was told to strike the rock in order to obtain water, so it seems reasonable to suppose that, in addition to speaking, he might strike it this time also.

There was something much more important, I believe, than striking or not striking the rock. We had better look at the passage itself,

"And the Lord said to Moses, Take the rod, and assemble the congregation, you and Aaron your brother, and tell the rock before their eyes to yield its water; so you shall bring water out of the rock for them; so you shall give drink to the congregation and their cattle. And Moses took the rod from before the Lord, as he commanded him. And Moses and Aaron gathered the assembly together before the rock, and he said to them,"hear now, you rebels; shall we bring forth water for you out of the rock?" And Moses lifted up his hand and struck the rock with his rod twice; and water came forth abundantly, and the congregation drank, and their cattle. And the Lord said to Moses and Aaron, "Because you did not believe in me, to sanctify me in the eyes of the people of Israel, therefore you shall not bring this assembly into the land which I have given them."" (Numbers 20:7-12 KJV).

Whenever any of the great miracle workers of Old or New Testament, Joseph, Daniel, or Paul, performed a mighty act, they were careful to say, "I cannot interpret dreams, (heal cripples, or whatever) but

God can." Man must acknowledge that God alone has the power. Moses said, "Shall we bring forth water?" Now whether he meant "Aaron and I" by "we" or "God and I," he was not being meek. He was not giving honor where honor is due, so he must take his punishment. He had succumbed to the besetting temptation of all leaders.

This was only one incident in his life, however, and we have another example of his meekness right at the end of his life. Moses is allowed to go up on a mountain to look into the Promised Land. He then asks God if he can go into the Land, and God says, "That is enough,...Do not speak to me anymore about this matter." (Deut. 3:26, NIV). Then, in spite of this disappointment Moses asks God to appoint a leader so the people will not flounder during the transition (Numbers 27:12-23). These rebellious people who have given Moses such a hard time for forty years are going to get to go into the Promised Land and Moses is not. Yet he loves them so much that he is concerned about their welfare at this difficult time in his own life. He was humble, he did not have his mind on himself, so he was able to love others.

We must be humble in order to be able to love. But how do we attain humility? I believe that Moses' life answers that question also. Moses had seen God in a way that no one else in the Old Testament had seen him (Ex. 33:18-33), and that made all the difference. Lewis said, "The real test of being in the presence of God is that you either forget about yourself altogether or see yourself as a small dirty object. It is better to forget about yourself altogether."[4]

Francis Schaeffer has a Christmas sermon entitled "What Difference Has Looking Made?" In it he tells about the shepherds getting a glimpse of heaven in seeing and hearing the angels sing and then seeing God in the baby Jesus. Then he says, "It is difficult to imagine the shepherds quarreling about personal prerogatives. I cannot imagine being faced with the glory of heaven and the Savior of the world and then say to someone else, 'I'm first, fellow, I'm first.'"[5] His point is that if we see God, it will make a difference in how we treat others.

There is an excellent example of what getting a vision of God does in the book of Job. During his troubles, Job is sorely perplexed about why God is allowing all of this to happen to him. He does not understand God. He does understand his "comforters" and has absolutely no ambivalence toward them. To say the least, he is upset with them. He tells them, "Sorry comforters are you all" (16:2). "How long will you torment me, and crush me with words? These ten times you have insulted me. You are not ashamed to wrong me." In fact he, uses sometimes subtle and clever sarcasm against them.

Then in the last chapter God tells Job to pray for their forgiveness. Think of it, after the agony they caused him, he now had to pray for them. Human nature would say no, let them suffer a little. But Job had seen God so he was able to love even his "sorry comforters." He did not need to get a good self-image. He needed to see God. All the way through the book he seems to have had a fairly good self-image. It was a vision of God that he needed. After receiving that vision he said, "I have heard of Thee by the hearing of the ear; but now my eye sees Thee; therefore I retract, and I repent in dust and ashes." After seeing God, I believe he had no trouble praying for his "comforters."

There are some passages in Philippians that summarize this relationship between humility and love. In Philippians 2:2-11, Paul encourages the Christians at Philippi to be "of the same mind maintaining the same love, united in spirit, intent on one purpose." That is, he is encouraging them to have the kind of unity that Christ had prayed for. In verses 3 and 4, he cautions them not to be selfish, but in humility to consider one another more important than themselves. Then in verses 5-11, he says look at Christ Jesus and have the same attitude of humility and submission He had when He left heaven to enter this world as a man and then even to suffer death on a cross.

Back in Jesus' prayer in John 17, after He prayed for our unity so that the world would know that God loved them, He prayed that the disciples might behold His glory. John 17:24-27,
> "Father, I want those you have given me to be with me where
> I am, and to see my glory, the glory you have given me be-

cause you loved me before creation of the world. Righteous Father, though the world does not know you, I know you, and these men know that you have sent me. I have revealed you to them, and will continue to make you known in order that the love you have for me may be theirs and that I myself may be in them." (NIV)

Notice that He promises to continue to make God known to us in order that we might have God's love in us. Once we have seen God (and it is easier for us to see God than it was for Job because since Job's time, Christ came into our world), then we can see our fellow men well enough to love them. Moses had seen God and his fellow Israelites well enough that he was willing to give his life for them. That is, he was willing either to die in their place or to live sacrificially serving them.

In Matthew 11:28-30, Jesus says, "Come unto me, all ye that labor and are heavy laden, and I will give you rest. Take my yoke upon you, and learn of me; for I am meek and lowly in heart: and ye shall find rest unto your souls. For my yoke is easy, and my burden is light" (KJV). We need to come to Jesus, study Him, really see Him. Then we will learn meekness and so obtain rest. As long as we are thinking about ourselves, comparing ourselves with others, competing with others, we are miserable. When we get our minds off of ourselves, we find rest and happiness. I have found that some of my most miserable times occurred when I was concerned about whether I was as good a teacher as someone else, as good a father, or even, as ridiculous as it may be, when I was concerned about whether I could bowl as well or play ping-pong as well as someone else.

Lewis says that we must be humble, not because God is concerned about His dignity, but because it is best for us.

The point is, He wants you to know Him: wants to give you Himself. And He and you are two things of such a kind that if you really get into any kind of touch with Him you will, in fact, be humble—delightedly humble, feeling the infinite relief of having for once got rid of all the silly nonsense about your own dignity which has made you restless and unhappy all your life.[6]

A character in a Tolstoy novel illustrates this. Dimitri used to have to devise things to do, which always centered round one and the same person—Dimitri; and yet, notwithstanding the fact that all the interests of life had Dimitri as their pivot he was bored with all of them. Now everything he did concerned other people, and not Dimitri, and they were, all interesting and absorbing.[7]

As Thomas Merton says of the humble, "Having given up all desire to compete with other men, they suddenly wake up and find the joy of God is everywhere."[8] "It is impossible to overestimate the value of true humility and its power in the spiritual life. For the beginning of humility is the perfection of all joy."[9]

Our society does not understand the virtue of humility at all. Commercials encourage us to think about ourselves and to satisfy every whim. More than half a century ago, G. K. Chesterton recognized the danger of commercialism and publicity or public relations. "We have heard something, and we ought to hear more, of modern capitalism and commercialism reversing the Christian idea of charity to the poor. But we have not heard much about advertisement, with its push, publicity and self-assertion, reversing the idea of Christian humility."[10]

In summary, before we can love, we must be humble. To be humble, we must see God. We can get glimpses of God in nature and in the lives of good people, especially people who are actively cooperating with God to grow into the fullness of the stature of Christ. But most of all we can see God by learning about the man Jesus. In his humanity is the best revelation of God. Then as we see God more clearly we become more humble, are able to love better, and become truly happy.

Logical Love

"If God is one eternal Spirit, completely loving,
and if we are akin to Him, even remotely,
it is our high destiny to be loving, too."

Elton Trueblood

In the fall of 1977, I was preparing to teach a course I had entitled "Love and Logic." My teen-age daughter exclaimed that those two things were not consistent with each other. When I asked her to explain what she meant, she said, "For example, it isn't logical to forgive people who have done something very nasty to you." Then after a short pause, "Unless you love them." I think her answer is profound and suggests the answer to the question, "Is it logical to love?"

To try to answer that question we need to look carefully and logically at a few important passages on love. In Luke 10, a lawyer or teacher of the law, in order to test Jesus, asked, "What shall I do to inherit eternal life?" Jesus wisely replied, "What do you understand the law to say about this?" The law professor could not resist giving the correct answer: "You shall love the Lord your God with all your strength, and with all your mind, and your neighbor as yourself." Jesus agrees that this statement of the two great commandments is indeed the answer to his question. The teacher of the law, realizing that he appears in an awkward light to the crowds by answering so easily his own question quickly adds, "Yes, but who is my neighbor? That is the difficult word to define." Jesus defines it beautifully in the story of the Good Samaritan as anyone who needs help that we are able to supply.

There are many interesting aspects to this passage in Luke, but the most crucial for our purpose right now is that from his study of the Old Testament the lawyer knew the importance of these commandments. Many people think that these commands to love are Jesus' unique insight and contribution to theology. Of course, Jesus did emphasize them, but the Old Testament contains them. "And you shall love the Lord your God with all your heart, and with all your soul, and with all your might" (Deut. 6:5). "... love your neighbor as yourself: I am the Lord" (Lev. 19:18). The preceding nine verses clarify what it means to love others. Strangers were to be included as neighbors according to Lev. 19:34: "The stranger who sojourns with you shall be to you as the native among you, and you shall love him as yourself; for you were strangers in the land of Egypt: I am the Lord your God." You might notice that God gives reasons for this command. It is logical for them to love because they were once in need of love, and God who has shown himself to be a God of love commands them to do so.

It is clear then that we should love our fellow men as ourselves and that this is commanded in the Old Testament. In John 13:34, Jesus says, "A new commandment I give unto you that ye love one another..." How can it be a <u>new</u> commandment to love one another? The Old Testament, as we have seen, clearly teaches this also. One of my axioms is that Jesus always speaks truly and logically. The explanation is in the last part of John 13:34. I left off the last part of the verse in order to emphasize it now. "A new commandment I give unto you that ye love one another; <u>even as I have loved you</u>, that you also love one another." This is amazing! The new part is that we are to go beyond loving our neighbor as ourselves. We are to love as Christ loved us. There are two levels of love here, both very high levels, but the second is higher than the first. Sometimes I am content with the second best (even third or fourth) for myself. For example, I might know that my welfare is best served by not eating a second piece of pie, but I settle for less than the best and eat that second piece. However, Jesus never is satisfied with second best; He always wants what is best for me.

In one of his sermons, George MacDonald gives a good description of how Jesus loves.

> But as the love of Him who is love, transcends ours as the heavens are higher than the earth, so must He desire in His child infinitely more than the most jealous love of the best mother can desire in hers. He would have him rid of all fear, all grudging, all bitterness in word or thought, all gauging and measuring of his own with a different rod from that he would apply to another's. He will have no curling of the lip; no indif-

ference in him to the man whose service in any form he uses; no desire to excel another, no contentment at gaining by his loss. He will not have him receive the smallest service without gratitude; would not hear from him a tone to jar the heart of another, a word to make it ache, be the ache ever so transient.[1]

I am indebted to Juan Carlos Ortiz for this insight into different levels of love. I strongly recommend his book, _A Call to Discipleship_. It is difficult to discuss the distinction between these two levels because it may appear that I feel that the first level is easy or at least that I have mastered it, neither of which is true. It is very difficult to love one's neighbor as oneself. Nevertheless, I believe that some non-Christians attain this level fairly consistently. Abraham Lincoln may be an example of this. He might correctly be classified as a Christian in the last few years of his life, but certainly most of his life he could not be. Yet, his philosophy was to give in to others in small things even if he had the greater right and in great matters even if he had an equal right. In other words, he would fight for his own rights only in those cases where the matter was very important and his own right was the greater right. It could be thought that he only claimed this philosophy but did not live it. However, I believe his life showed it. As examples, you might check his conduct in the Illinois senatorial election of 1855, which was won by Lyman Trumbull even though Lincoln had the greater claim to that position; and Lincoln's treatment of Edwin Stanton in 1862 after Stanton's treatment of Lincoln in a law case in 1855.

On the other hand, I believe that George Washington Carver's treatment of prejudiced white men goes beyond even this high level of love to the second level of loving others as Christ loved them. Carver was a scientist who, among other accomplishments, found many ways to use the peanut and better methods of farming. He shared these ideas with farmers in the southern part of the United States and thus helped them to improve their financial well being. The amazing thing about his sharing is that he shared these ideas with the white farmers even when they treated him as an inferior. For example, at banquets at which he would be the after dinner speaker but he would not be allowed to sit down and eat with them. Loving others as Christ loved us is impossible on a human level and can only be done through the power of the Holy Spirit. Still, it is the new command that Jesus gave us.

Paul also teaches that love of self is not to be the measure of our love for others. "Do nothing from selfishness or conceit, but in humility count others better than yourselves" (Phil. 2:4). "We who are strong ought to bear with the failings of the weak, and not to please ourselves; let each of us please his neighbor for his good, to edify him" (Rom. 15:1-2). As the Swedish theologian Anders Nygren says in his in-depth study of love, *Agape and Eros*,

> Nothing is more alien to his (Paul's) mind than to base neighborly love on a 'spiritual' self-love, as though the ego must first look after its own spiritual interests and then secondarily show love to its neighbor. No; Christian love must be ready, according to Paul, to sacrifice even its 'spiritual' advantages and privileges, if need be, in the service of its neighbor.[2]

Not only does the New Testament demand a deeper love than the Old Testament demands, as Ortiz has pointed out, but also a broader love. In Matthew 5:43-48 and Luke 6:31-35, Jesus clearly states that we are to love our enemies also. That aspect of love was not so clearly understood in the Old Testament times. Leviticus 19:34 included strangers as well as brothers and neighbors but that is still not the same as enemies. I think there is a hint of the need for love for enemies in Prov. 24:17 and 18. In any case, it is an extremely interesting passage. Verse 17 says, "Do not rejoice when your enemy falls; and let not your heart be glad when he stumbles." This would be more clear and positive if it were not for verse 18, which adds, "Lest the Lord see it, and be displeased, and turn away his anger from him." It almost seems as though we are to hide our elation from God lest he stop punishing our enemy! I doubt that it means exactly that. Whatever its complete meaning is, I think that it is at least some indication that God is displeased with us if we hate our enemies. Also, in Ezekiel 18:23 we find, "'Do I take any pleasure in the death of the wicked?' declares the Sovereign Lord.

'Rather, am I not pleased when they turn from their ways and live?'"
There are some examples of love to enemies in the Old Testament,
such as Joseph's kind treatment of his brothers after they had sold him
into slavery and some had even wanted to kill him (Gen. 45: 5-15 and
50:19-21). David's treatment of Saul, in spite of repeated attempts on
Saul's part to kill David, is another example (I Sam. 24:10-12; 26:9,
23; and II Sam. 1:14-17).

Jesus' command to love our enemies does not seem to be emphasized in the epistles, although Paul writes in I Thessalonians 3:12, "and
may the Lord make you increase and abound in love to one another and
to all men, as we do to you." The emphasis seems to be on love for the
brethren but all men are included. Perhaps this is because the place to
begin is to love those nearest us. If we can't love our neighbors, how
can we love our enemies?

Still, the command is to love our enemies. The parable of the Good
Samaritan shows a love for enemies since the Jews and Samaritans
certainly did not consider themselves to be brethren. And we do have
examples of love for enemies in the New Testament. Paul expresses
concern, love, and willingness to sacrifice greatly for the benefit of the
Jews (Rom. 9:1-3). Now it is true that these were his kinsmen, but
their opposition to Paul would qualify them for the status of enemies
by the world's standards. I'm sure they considered themselves to be
Paul's enemies.

The supreme example of love for enemies is Jesus' prayer for those
crucifying him: "Father, forgive them; for they know not what they
do" (Luke 23:34). We might have thought that no one but Jesus could
love like that, but there is a similar incident recorded in Acts 7:60.
While Stephen is being stoned and about to die, he cries in a loud voice,
"Lord do not hold this sin against them." The Holy Spirit has enabled
other Christians to have this kind of love. One example is Dirk Willems
in the sixteenth century. Many of Dirk's fellow Anabaptists had been
put to death for their faith, and Dirk was fleeing from men who would
most likely kill him if they caught him. He fled across the thin ice on

a river and seemed to have escaped for the moment when he heard one of his pursuers, who had broken through the ice, call for help. "Dirk immediately turned back and managed to rescue him, but on orders of the burgomaster on the other side of the river, the man he saved arrested him on the spot. He was burned at the stake on May 16, 1569, paying for this deed of mercy with his life."[3]

A twentieth century example of love for one's enemy is Festo Kivengere. After terrible persecution of the Christians in Uganda by Idi Amin, Bishop Kivengere wrote an amazing little book entitled *I Love Idi Amin*. It wasn't easy. As Kivengere says, the Holy Spirit pointed out his need to love, and he had to pray for strength to do it. But God answered his prayer so he was able to say, "We love President Idi Amin. We owe him the debt of love, for he is one of those for whom Christ shed his precious blood. As long as he is alive he is still redeemable. Pray for him, that in the end he may see a new way of life, rather than a way of death."[4] He also says that love always costs something. "For the love of Christ was demonstrated through suffering, and those who experience that love can never put it into practice without some cost."[5]

This command to love our enemies destroys all bounds as to whom we love just as the command to love as Jesus loves destroys all bounds to the extent of how we love. Tolstoy shows us how a lack of understanding of what love is causes us difficulty in understanding how we can love even our enemies. He comments about someone that "she cannot understand love for one's enemies… She, and many others, do not understand it, mainly because they think that the partiality they feel for other people is love."[6]

I have referred to only a few brief New Testament passages on love. The entire New Testament, I believe, amply supports these extreme (from a human standpoint) conclusions about the nature of love that is demanded from a Christian. It is only on the assumption that the reader is familiar with the New Testament that we can return to the question of whether it is logical to love. Whether a conclusion is valid or not valid depends upon the premises. Whether it is logical to love or not depends upon our basic beliefs, our premises.

A Christian accepts the Bible as God's word, so it contains our basic beliefs. Since the Sermon on the Mount tells us to love our enemies, to be meek, to go the second mile, etc., these must be our premises. From a purely human standpoint, the Sermon on the Mount seems impractical. However, God would not command it unless it was practical. It is only possible by God's grace, but God's grace is one of the Christian's axioms.

The story of Bob and Golden Bristol illustrates the logic of Christian love and gives us a modern day example of love for enemies. The twenty-year-old daughter of this couple from Dearborn, Michigan was raped and brutally murdered in 1970. Michael Keeyes was convicted of this murder and imprisoned in California. Mr. and Mrs. Bristol traveled from Michigan to California to see Keeyes and speak to the inmates at the prison. Mrs. Bristol said that when they received the news about their daughter's rape and murder "it cut like a knife into the depth of our souls. We had the normal human reaction of grief and anguish." However, Golden Bristol said of Michael Keeyes "We love this special person from the bottom of our hearts."[7] On purely humanistic or naturalistic axioms it would not be logical to love the murderer of one's daughter. Certainly, everyone's emotions would be commanding hate not love. But a Christian's axioms include: God is a loving God, He is completely in charge of everything in the universe, and this life is not the end. On Christian axioms, it is logical to forgive and to love. Mrs. Bristol said, "We harbored no hatred, no revenge. We knew God could make something good out of this pain." And then added, "What would make us happiest is when he (Keeyes) accepts Jesus Christ."

When I say that it is logical for a Christian to love even in difficult situations like this, it should be kept in mind that I do not mean it is easy to love. Christians have emotions like other people, and when someone hurts us, our emotions make it extremely difficult to love. It is important to be aware that emotion not logic causes the difficulty.

Many people believe that logic is cold and cruel while emotions are warm and kind; and thus, the heart (or emotions) should always rule the head (or logic). This is simply not true. Emotions are sometimes good, sometimes evil. For a Christian, it is hard to forgive for emotional reasons, not logical reasons. Remember that conclusions are valid or not depending on the axioms. If we start with non-Christian axioms, it might be logical to not love.

Another Christian axiom is that the Christian has been crucified with Christ. To bear one's cross means to die. Our wills are crucified. Only thus is it possible to sincerely (and logically) desire the welfare of another and be willing to personally work and sacrifice for that welfare. Statements like "You have to stand up for your own rights" have emotional appeal but are not logical, starting from Christian axioms.

It is obvious that, at least sometimes, it is very difficult to love. Some have said that agape is really impossible for humans, that it is against human nature. E. Stanley Jones has considered carefully this problem. He asks,

> Is love central in us? In the very make-up of our being? Are we made by love for love, and can we live without it? Is the demand for love not merely written in the Scriptures, but is that same demand written in us?… If Christianity and the most basic demands of human nature are at cross purposes, demanding opposite things, then we are in trouble—deep trouble, life trouble. But if they turn out to be the same, then we can be all-out Christians."[8]

If agape were not at the heart of my nature, then it would be impossible for me to keep Christ's command to love. But John says, "For this is the love of God, that we keep his commandments, and his commandments are not burdensome" (I John 5:3). This gives the final answer, but Paul supplies more of the details. "For I delight in the law of God in my inmost self, but I see in my members another law at war with the law of my mind and making me captive to the law of sin which dwells in my members" (Romans 7:22-23). Paul here makes the claim that agape is "in my inmost self." But there is another force at war with this. Where does this other force come from? Man was made in the image of God. God's basic nature is love. Therefore man's basic nature was love. But there has been a Fall. Jones says that our primary nature is to love, but as a result of the fall there is a second nature, called original sin, which has grown strong within us. Notice that it is called original sin, not original nature. This second nature has taken hold of us so that it seems that it is basic, but it is not. If it were our basic nature, then we would die when it died. In Colossians 2:20 Paul says that with Christ we die "to the elemental spirits of the universe." These elemental spirits of the universe have made us dead through trespasses and sins. Ephesians 2 tells us that these spirits are at work in "the sons of disobedience," but the Christian has been made alive. The cross, which is a symbol of God's love for us, is also a symbol of the death of our secondary (sinful) nature when we are crucified with Christ. Only thus can our primary self again exert itself and we "become alive," having again the capability to love as Christ loved us.

Modern psychology has come to this same conclusion, that love is not contrary to our basic nature, but, in fact, is essential for our well-being. Dr. M. Boss, who was a professor of psychotherapy at the University of Zurich and President of the International Psychiatric Association, claimed that love was the basic urge in human personality. He also said, "When I first began my psychiatry I had a battle to put Christian faith and psychiatry together. But the demands of human nature brought me back to Christianity."[9] Karl Menninger's book _Love Against Hate_ and Smiley Blanton's _Love or Perish_ are further examples of psychology's discovery of love as an essential need in human nature. It seems that modern psychology agrees with the Bible on the fundamental nature of love. Thus the secondary sinful nature can be destroyed without destroying us. In fact, when the secondary sinful nature is destroyed, our primary nature makes it possible, as well as logical for us to love.

With his great novelist's insight, Tolstoy has come to the same conclusion.

The whole trouble is that people think there are circumstances when one may deal with human beings without love, but no such circumstances ever exist. Inanimate objects may be dealt with without love: we may fell trees, bake bricks, hammer iron without love. But human beings cannot be handled without love, any more than bees can be handled without care. That is the nature of bees. If you handle bees carelessly you will harm the bees and yourself as well. And so it is with people. And it cannot be otherwise, because mutual love is the fundamental law of human life."[10]

Thomas Merton puts it this way, "To say that I am made in the image of God is to say that love is the reason for my existence: for God is love. Love is my true identity. Selflessness is my true self. Love is my true character."[11]

In the old familiar hymn "When I Survey the Wondrous Cross" by Isaac Watts are the lines, "Love so amazing, so divine, Demands my soul, my life, my all." It is because of God's amazing love that we should love. As a valid inference logically demands that I accept its conclusion, so the amazing love of God ethically demands that I give Him my soul, my life, my all and means loving my neighbor as myself.

It is logical for a Christian to love others. In fact, it is a complete break with reason not to. C. S. Lewis, in a powerful passage describes how certain Christian axioms lead naturally and necessarily to a real and costly love:

It may be possible for each to think too much of his own potential glory hereafter; it is hardly possible for him to think too often or too deeply about that of his neighbor. The load, or weight, or burden of my neighbor's glory should be laid daily on my back, a load so heavy that only humility can carry it, and the backs of the proud will be broken. It is a serious thing to live in a "society of possible gods and goddesses, to remember that the dullest and most uninteresting person you talk to may one day be a creature which, if you saw it now, you would be strongly tempted to worship, or else a horror and a corruption such as you now meet, if at all, only in a nightmare. All day long we are, in some degree, helping each other to one or other of these destinations. It is in the light of these overwhelming possibilities, it is with the awe and the circumspection proper to them, that we should conduct all our dealings with one another, all friendships, all loves, all play, all politics. There are no ordinary people. You have never talked to a mere mortal. Nations, cultures, arts, civilizations—these are mortal, and their life is to ours as the life of a gnat. But it is immortals whom we joke with, work with, marry, snub and exploit—immortal horrors or everlasting splendors. This does not mean that we are to be perpetually solemn. We must play. But our merriment must be of that kind (and it is, in fact, the merriest kind) which exists between people who have, from the outset, taken each other seriously—no flippancy, no superiority, no presumption. And our charity must be a real and costly

Love, with deep feeling for the sins in spite of which we love the sinner—not mere tolerance or indulgence which parodies love as flippancy parodies merriment."[12]

Love and Knowledge

"He who loves, sees."
George MacDonald

We have seen that love needs reason and knowledge in order to be effective. Thus love often provides motivation to seek knowledge. Logic, of course, is a tool that is useful in acquiring knowledge. So we have both love and logic as aids in the path to knowledge. The aim of this chapter, though, is to explore the possibility of a more intimate relation between love and knowledge than simply that love is a motivating force. One hint that there is a closer relationship is the Old Testament use of the word "know" when referring to the sexual act between husband and wife.

To be specific, I hope to show that love, in some instances, is an important aspect of coming to have knowledge. In fact, for some kinds of knowledge it is a prerequisite. In this way it is parallel to logic, as logic or deductive reasoning is essential in obtaining some kinds of knowledge. It is not that there are only two paths to knowledge, one by way of logic without love and the other via love without logic, but that there are many paths to knowledge each depending more or less on both love and logic.

In the song "Day by Day" from the musical *Godspell*, a daily prayer is expressed, "To love Thee more dearly, To see Thee more clearly, To follow Thee more nearly." I believe that these are not three independent requests, but that each is closely connected with the other two. If we love God more, then we will see (know) Him better and follow (obey) Him more nearly. Also, if we get to know Him better, we will love and obey Him more. Finally, if we follow Him more nearly (that is, obey Him in those areas where we understand what is required of us), then we will love Him more and know Him better.

"To know me is to love me," is a statement you have probably heard someone say. For most of us, it is not an obvious truth. Although at a deeper level, it probably is true that if we really know someone and understand that he is made in the image of God, we may not always admire him in his present condition, but we will love him. In any case, I believe that to know God is to love Him.

In the chapter on the meaning of love, obedience to God was shown to result from love, but perhaps it would be wise to consider it again here. Joshua 22:5 says, "Take good care to observe the commandment and the law which Moses the servant of the Lord commanded you, to love the Lord your God, and to serve him with all your heart and with all your soul." (See also, Deut. 11:1, 13, 22 and I John 5:3.) John 14:15 states the relation clearly and concisely, "If you love me, you will keep my commandments." Then in verses 16 and 17 Jesus adds "And I will pray the Father, and he will give you another Counselor, to be with you forever, even the Spirit of Truth whom the world cannot receive." This Spirit of Truth will teach us all things (John 14:26). Thus, love leads to obedience, and then to knowledge. The sequence is repeated in verse 21 of the same chapter. "He who has my commandments and keeps them, he it is who loves me; and he who loves me will be loved by my Father, and I will love him and manifest myself to him." Obeying His commandments is evidence of our love for Him and results in knowledge. ("I will...manifest myself to him.")

In John 7:17, Jesus says, "If any man's will is to do his will, he shall know whether the teaching is from God." That is, if we obey, then we obtain knowledge. Paul admonishes us to be true to what we know and God will reveal more (Phil. 3:15-16). The contrapositive, if we do not obey, then we do not understand, is expressed by Jesus in John 8:43-44. The converse, knowledge is given to us to bring about obedience, is found in Romans 16:25-26. Notice how Colossians 1:9-10 tells us that knowledge leads to obedience resulting in more knowledge. "And so, from the day we heard of it, we have not ceased to pray for you, asking that you may be filled with the knowledge of his will in all spiritual wisdom and understanding, to lead a life worthy of the Lord, fully pleasing to him, bearing fruit in every good work and increasing in the knowledge of God."

The idea of doing (obeying) preceding knowledge (I am using knowledge in its most general sense, which includes understanding) is illustrated in many day to day experiences. We might read about or be told how to do a certain task, but after we actually do it, we know much more about it and understand it better. For example, most people do not know why the method for long division works before they have used it many times. Many may never understand why it works, but those who do obeyed the rules at first without knowing why. Only later did the light dawn, and they understood the method.

Not only love of God, but also love of our brother enables us to live in the light, that is, see and know. "He who loves his brother abides in the light and in it there is no cause for stumbling. But he who hates his brother, is in the darkness and does not know where he is going, because the darkness has blinded his eyes" (I John 2:10-11). In II Peter 1: 6, Peter relates knowledge, obedience, and love when he tells us to try hard to add to our knowledge, virtue (obedience) and eventually also love.

Therefore, love, knowledge, and obedience are related in various ways. Maybe the best model of the relationship would be an ascending spiral. Knowledge leads to love, which leads to obedience, which leads to more knowledge, which leads to more love, and so on, around and up the spiral. We needn't worry about where or how the spiral began, just where we are on it and how best to continue our journey. Of course, God is the source of all of these. He gives us knowledge in various ways, but we must keep in mind we have a part to play also. He enables us to love and obey. Our part here is the setting of our wills (remember, love involves the will) and cooperating with God in obedience.

We have been considering primarily our knowledge and love of God; however, a similar relation occurs when we consider our love and knowledge of people, both on individual and group levels. First we need to consider what is often termed objective and subjective knowledge. By using these labels, it appears that there are two distinct kinds of knowledge. In reality there is an objective-subjective continuum. Nothing is all one or all the other. Objective means unbiased, existing in reality, not influenced or colored by the mind or the emotions of the observer. As we have seen in Part I, all facts are influenced by our views, hypotheses, and emotions so that nothing is purely objective. On the other hand, if we went to the subjective extreme we would have no knowledge at all.

To illustrate the relation between objective and subjective knowledge, consider two people, one a swimmer and the other a detached and careful observer of the swimmer. Suppose the observer has never swum but has made a scientific study of the procedures used in swimming while the swimmer, although a good and experienced swimmer, has never given much thought to the process. It should be clear that each has some knowledge of swimming, one from the outside (objective knowledge) and the other from the inside (subjective knowledge). I think that it is also obvious that neither type of knowledge could be said to be intrinsically better than the other. One might be more useful for some purposes than the other and vice versa.

As another, and more personal example, I have some knowledge of Mennonites. I am, myself, a Mennonite and have a special love for Mennonites. This does not mean that I love Mennonites more than other people. It just means that my commitment to this group is uniquely influenced by my identification with it. I have knowledge about Mennonites from various sources, for example, personal experience and study of Mennonite history. Even though I have read books by non-Mennonites about Mennonites, my knowledge about them must be considered subjective, from the inside.

My contention is that I have some knowledge of Mennonites that a non-Mennonite could never have. Love was an essential on that path to knowledge. Keep in mind that it is also true that a non-Mennonite might study Mennonites as objectively as he could and know things that I do not know. Or looked at another way, two non-Mennonite scholars might study Mennonites in two different ways, one as detached and objective as possible, the other as involved with them as he can be. The one will be more unbiased than the other, but at the end each may know some things the other does not know.

What is true at the group level becomes even more obvious at the individual level. I am sure that I know my wife better than any objective observer could know her, no matter how scientific his study might be. He might know some things I do not know and in fact, perhaps could never learn, but I would still know more that is important about her essential nature. In fact, because I love her deeply, I know her better than if we had been married for the same period of time but without love.

For some kinds of knowledge, particularly about people, love is essential. Even some kinds of knowledge about swimming seem to at least require a commitment to and participation in that activity.

Why is it that love is so intimately involved with knowledge? Is there something about us or about nature that requires love in order for us to know? I think there is. Remember that God is love and He created us as well as other people and the rest of the universe. Therefore, love is basic in all of nature, not just in human nature. Because of the Fall, our sinful natures are unloving, and nature itself is in "bondage to decay" (See Romans 8:19-23). But our basic nature in spite of the fall is loving, and Christ is able to restore that nature. All of creation is the expression of a loving God.

Thomas Merton said, "It was because the saints were absorbed in God that they were truly capable of seeing and appreciating created things."[1] This statement comes from a context where Merton is talking about loving God, and certainly, one could not really be absorbed in God without loving Him. So it is by loving God that we can see (i.e. know about) created things. It is only reasonable that we could understand the creation better by loving the Creator.

The reason we must love in order to understand another person is given by Washington Allston.

> No right judgment can ever be formed on any subject having a moral or intellectual bearing without benevolence; for so strong

is man's natural self-bias, that, without this restraining principle, he insensibly becomes a competitor in all such cases presented to his mind; and when the comparison is thus made personal, unless the odds be immeasurable against him, his decision will rarely be impartial. In other words, no one can see anything as it really is through the misty spectacles of self-love. We must wish well to another in order to do him justice. Now the virtue in this goodwill is not to blind us to his faults, but to our own rival and interposing merits.[2]

Therefore, in order to know and understand certain essential things about God, other people, and all of creation, we must, through love, come into contact with the love that is there. There is no other way to certain kinds of knowledge than the way of love. This is very likely the solution to our ecological problems. Man was told by God to subdue the earth. It appeared for a while that man's technology was doing that, but it is now evident that the earth may yet defeat man. Love was the missing ingredient and must be supplied. Certainly, Christians who are in touch with the source of love ought to be contributing most to setting things right between man and nature, between man and man, as well as between man and God.

So we have one more relationship between love and logic. Each is an aid in acquiring knowledge. The importance of love to knowledge is beautifully expressed by Carl Boberg in the Swedish hymn, "My Soul Now Magnifies The Lord."

"His wisdom cannot be discerned
By carnal minded man;
But he who truly loves the Lord
Shall know His sacred plan;
The man whose heart is filled with pride
Will God, the Lord, bring low;
To him who humbly serves his God
Shall streams of mercy flow."

More Relationships

"And earthly power doth them show likest God's,
When mercy seasons justice."

Shakespeare

In this chapter, we consider the relation of love to a variety of things that did not quite fit into previous chapters. We will consider fear, power, righteousness, justice, and law in relation to love. What I have to say about each of them does not merit a separate chapter. In other words, this is a chapter of odds and ends, although they are important odds and ends.

Just as the emotion of hate interferes with our ability to love, so does fear. "There is no fear in love, but perfect love casts out fear" (I John 4:18). Fear not only keeps us from loving but also from thinking clearly and it weakens us. "For God hath not given us the spirit of fear; but of power, and of love, and of a sound mind" (II Tim. 1:7 KJV). It is precisely because a Christian need not fear that it is possible for him to love, think clearly, and possess power. In _The Gulag Archipelago_, Solzenitzen expresses the opinion that the prisoner must die to self and give up all ideas of property or position (then fear would be gone), and only then could he have power and be able to think clearly. We might add, and also be able to love. Mr. Nunn, President of the NunnBush Company expressed the relationship between fear, reason, and love in the context of employer-employee negotiations thus: "When fear is removed from the human heart, reason enters. A man will not reason when he is out of temper or when his feelings are outraged by threats of arbitrary action. Concessions beget concessions and trust begets trust."[1] Not only is it true that where fear is removed, love and logic may enter, but also when we show love to another person ,it helps remove his fear enabling him to love in turn. Love begets love, but fear begets fear. On his own, man would be stuck in the fear begets fear cycle. But God has broken into that vicious cycle and by his love casts out our fear, enabling us to love and begin the love cycle.

Almost forty years ago, in a speech in New York, Alan Paton said, It is my own belief that the only power which can resist the power of fear is the power of love. It's a weak thing and a tender thing; men despise and deride it. But I look for the day when in South Africa we shall realize that the only lasting and worth-while solution of our grave and profound problems lies not in the use of power, but in that understanding and compassion without which human life is an intolerable bondage, condemning us all to an existence of violence, misery and fear.[2]

Unfortunately, that day when the power of love is realized has not yet fully come in South Africa, or in any other place in this world. However, Paton's novel, *Cry, The Beloved Country*, illustrates better and gives more insight into the nature of love than any novel I have ever read.

This power of love is something we must never forget. With it, God conquered all the power of sin, death, and hell. "Love never fails" (I Cor. 13:8, NIV). As Thomas Merton said, "by loving others we can make them good and lovable, in spite of themselves."[3] This may sound unbelievably naive and too easy, but remember, it is the Bible that says, "Love never fails." And, it certainly isn't easy. The cost for Jesus was suffering and death on a cross.

There is another thing that must be considered in a discussion of the logic of love and that is righteousness. Love and righteousness cannot be separated. God has both, and because of His integrity they must be related. George MacDonald has said that "His mercy is just and His justice is merciful."[4]

This relation between love and justice is illustrated in Dostoevsky's *Crime and Punishment*. I am indebted to Earl Palmer for calling this to my attention in his excellent book *Love Has Its Reasons*. It caused me to reread *Crime and Punishment* to learn what it tells us about love. We will come, eventually, to what it says about love and justice, but to fully understand that relationship we need to review the plot of the story. In so doing, we can learn more about love.

The main character, Raskolnikov, is a student, or former student, who is proud and self-centered. Because of his own need for money, he comes to the conclusion that there are extraordinary people with special privileges. "An 'extraordinary' man has the right...that is not an official right, but an inner right to decide in his own conscience to overstep...certain obstacles, and only in case it is essential for the practical fulfillment of his idea (sometimes, perhaps, of benefit to the whole of humanity.)"[5] Overstepping certain obstacles includes even murder, if necessary. He considers himself to be one of these extraordinary men and so murders two people to obtain money to further his own career. Early in the book, a character says that "compassion is forbidden nowadays by science itself."[6]

Many times, Raskolnikov gives sacrificially to help others. But there is an aloofness about him that continually keeps him from any interaction with other people. It seems to me that his mother's love for him has lacked the guidance of logic and has contributed to his extreme egoism. A detective, Petrovitch, is convinced that Raskolnikov is guilty of the murders but cannot obtain evidence to prove it. Raskolnikov confesses to Sonia (who loves him) that he committed the murders. She insists, immediately, that he repent and turn himself in to the police. Sonia understands that her love for him demands that he "stand at the crossroads, bow down, first kiss the earth which [he has] defiled and then bow down to all the world and say to all men aloud, 'I am a murderer!' Then God will send you life." As Norman Geisler has said, "The highest expression of concern for another human being is to will for them what God commands for them. And God commands them what He requires of all men, viz., that they take their place under God and not take the place of God."[7] This is love on Sonia's part in that she wants Raskolnikov to experience life again, and he can only do so by acknowledging his sin and his rightful place under God. Her love is Christlike in that she does not force or manipulate him or even turn him in herself. But eventually her "insatiable compassion" (Dostoevsky's beautiful term) convinces him to confess his crime to the police, although at that time he still denies feeling any personal guilt. He is then sentenced to serve an eight year term of imprisonment in Siberia. At this point, the detective is satisfied that justice has been done and turns his attention to other cases. But here Sonia shows another aspect of agape by going to Siberia to help him in whatever ways she can. Not incidentally, she helps many other prisoners as well.

Love and justice each demanded that Raskolnikov accept his punishment. But love and justice each demand a further interest in him as well, even in his suffering. Here is where Petrovich's concept of justice is defective. Even a murderer is made in the image of God, and Christ's death on the cross was for him. Therefore, Raskolnikov still deserves love. Raskolnikov does not believe that he deserves love and even that it is "painful to be so loved."[8] But, finally, Sonia's love for him in Siberia breaks his pride and his will, and he accepts his rightful place under God.

Love and law do not contradict each other. One is not even independent of the other. Law is the description of love. Love is the summary and the fulfilling of the law. The first four of the Ten Commandments help us to understand what it means to love God; the last six, what it means to love our neighbor. "Owe no one anything, except to love one another; for he who loves his neighbor has fulfilled the law. The commandments 'You shall not commit adultery, You shall not kill, You shall not covet,' and any other commandment, are summed up in this sentence, 'You shall love your neighbor as yourself.' Love does no wrong to a neighbor; therefore love is the fulfilling of the law" (Romans 13:8-10, see also Gal. 5:14 and James 2:8.).

How can we know what the way of righteousness demands in any given situation? Is there even "the way of righteousness?" C. S. Lewis gives a defense of moral law in *The Abolition of Man*. For our present discussion, I will assume that right and wrong exist. Ethical principles are necessary for guidance in daily life. Some principles may follow logically from others. As Paul says, "You shall not kill" follows logically from "You shall love your neighbor as yourself." But just as in mathematics not every statement can be a theorem - some must be axioms; likewise, in ethical theory some ethical statements must be basic and stand on their own. Lewis comments on this necessity of some basic ethical assumptions.

> Unless you accept these {basic assumptions] without question as being to the world of action what axioms are to the world of theory, you can have no practical principles whatever. You cannot reach them as conclusions: they are premises...you may...regard them as rational—nay as rationality itself—as things so obviously reasonable that they neither demand nor admit proof.[9]

This sounds like the Greek mathematicians' description of axioms as self-evident truths.

Mathematicians no longer consider their axioms as self-evident truths. They are just assumptions. This does not mean that a mathematician denies the existence of truth, only that within a mathematical system, because of the difficulty of agreeing on truth, axioms are simply designated as assumptions. I believe it is because of the Fall that man has trouble recognizing self-evident truths. It is much harder to secure universal agreement on basic ethical principles than on mathematical axioms. It makes sense to me that this should be so, since righteousness is closer to the essence of God than is logic. Therefore, the fall was greater for man in the area of ethics than in the area of logic. The rules of logic are not so obviously in conflict with our sinful pride as the ethical laws are.

The basic ethical axiom for Kant was the categorical imperative. That is, whatever decision I make for myself must be capable of being made a universal law for all men without contradiction. It is similar to the Golden Rule. For the Christian, the ethical axioms are the first and second commandments as given by Jesus. Perhaps the second even follows from the first. The rest follows logically from those, but God does not leave us to draw all of the implications ourselves. The whole Bible and especially the life and teachings of Christ show us many of the implications. It is good that we have that extra help. Isaac Newton wondered why the theorems for geometry needed to be written out since they are obvious, logical implications from the postulates. However, Newton was a genius. Most of us are not. It would be disastrous to try to teach geometry to an average high school sophomore by giving him a minimum set of axioms, as formulated by David Hilbert or some other mathematician. Most high school students need much more than the basic assumptions. They need lots of help in developing the subject to discover the implications of the axioms. In the same way, it is fortunate for us that we have the Old Testament to show us how God taught His chosen people some of the implications of the law of love, the New Testament to tell us how Jesus Christ taught and lived the law of love, and the Holy Spirit to continue to teach us what it means in every situation we must face.

Part III
Obedience & Implications

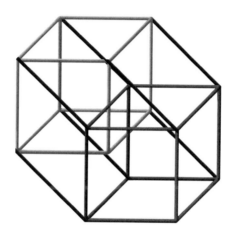

"We do not become saved by keeping the Law; we can only keep the Law because we are saved. All is of love, and a man cannot accept God's grace, and then go on to break the heart of the God who loved him so much."

William Barclay

Introduction

*"The withholding of love is the negation of the spirit of
Christ, the proof that we never knew Him."*

Henry Drummond

The only logical thing to do, if one knows God and loves Him, is to
obey Him. If one knows and loves a three-year-old, it is not logical to
obey everything that the three-year-old says. But God is a Being for
whom the only logical conclusion is obedience. The Creator of the
universe and everything in it is all-knowing, all-wise, all-powerful, and
all-loving. He knows what is best for us. He desires what is best for
us. Why shouldn't we obey Him? And remember, the greatest commandment is love.

The reason we would not obey a three-year-old that we knew and
loved is that the three year old would ask for many things that would
be harmful, not in his or her own best interest. Actually, if we know
and love any person, we would obey any commands that would promote the loved one's welfare. God knows what is best, not just for
Him but for us as well. And, he communicates with us through the
Bible, the Holy Spirit, and the community of believers.

This obedience is not just important, it is essential. Not that obedience leads to salvation; Paul and James are agreed upon that. In fact,
just the opposite. Salvation leads to obedience. Paul and James agree
upon that, also. Grace is not a cover-up for our sins. It is a power for
overcoming our sins.

Therefore, this section contains a chapter on grace followed by
chapters on the need for changed lives and the nature of the changed
life. Then there is a chapter on how and what love implies about community, that is, how people who are changed by the grace of God relate
to each other. In the chapter on pacifism, we will consider the implications of agape on the problems of war and violence.

The final chapter is a summary. As indicated earlier, the words of
a song from "Godspell" provide an outline for this treatment of reason

in religion.

> Day by day
> Three things I pray,
> To see Thee more clearly
> To love Thee more dearly
> To follow Thee more nearly.

Part I considers faith or knowledge of God, that is, to see Him more clearly. Part II is on love and Part III is on obedience or following Him. Progress in any one of these areas leads logically and automatically to progress in the others and so on in an ever increasing spiral toward that perfection that Jesus commands in the Sermon on the Mount.

Magic, Mirage, or Miracle

*"To Paul grace is the power which enables men to meet with
gallantry and with adequacy the demands, the responsibilities
and the tasks of this life."*

William Barclay

Magic, mirage, or miracle - which of these words best describes
the Christian life? Strange as it may seem, I believe that these three
words describe three different ways of looking at Christianity. And the
difference is of the utmost importance. We must start with the definitions of these words. At least we must understand the way I am using
them. Basically, these definitions are from Bible dictionaries and
Webster's.

A mirage is an illusion, something that falsely appears to be true.
Magic is a human being's use of incantations, charms, spells, formulas, etc. to control things, spirits, or people in a way advantageous to
one's self. A miracle is a wonderful, powerful, meaningful act of God,
beyond man's control or understanding, but in harmony with God's
nature. Please keep these meanings in mind as I use these words.

To non-Christians, Christianity seems to be a mirage. At times,
even Christians are tempted to doubt the reality of their faith. However, the danger I want to consider now is the view that Christianity is
magic, something that I can use to control people or nature for my own
benefit.

While my wife and I were in Brazil visiting our son and daughter-
in-law, we were in a museum and saw a roomful of clay and wooden
models of various parts of the human body. People who had sore toes,
headaches, stomachaches, or whatever would make a model of the ail-
ing part of the body and give these to God in return for healing. This
seemed to me to be a belief in magic. In the Old Testament we have
another example of the belief in magic. In the time when Eli was high
priest and Samuel was a boy, the elders of Israel decided to send the
Ark of the Covenant along with the army that was going to fight the

Philistines, with the magical hope that God would defeat Israel's enemies. It didn't work. The army was defeated, Eli's sons were killed, the Ark was captured, and Eli died. Miraculous events did take place in the Philistine cities, but Israel's fortunes did not change until Samuel led a nationwide revival.

Recently, a letter came to our house addressed to "Rural Route Boxholder." Inside was an offer for us to obtain a free "Prosperity Faith Grace Cross." All we had to do was return a postcard to receive this cross that could be worn as a necklace. We were told that it had been "blessed with prayer for your spiritual, physical and financial blessings." It was clear that the emphasis was on the financial blessings (e.g. money, cars, houses, appliances.) We were also told, "We have prayed over every word in this letter before we mailed it to your address. We have felt the Holy Spirit leading us to pray for somebody at this address." This seemed very strange since it had been mailed to rural route boxholder! This, of course, is an extreme example of what I mean by the magic view of Christianity. But I fear that, in less extreme forms, it is all too common today. So many people look at Christianity as a magic wand to bring them whatever they want. "After all," they say, "God wants what is best for His children." That is true, but they define what is best as material things, not remembering all the warnings in the Bible against the dangers of wealth.

This "magic view" seems to be growing among evangelicals today, and I believe it is a harmful view. It is the belief that all one needs to do to insure his eternal salvation is to say "I believe in Jesus Christ" and that there is no need to turn one's entire life over to Him. Words are easy to say. Sometimes it is even easy to think that we believe what we say. But saving faith is much more than intellectual assent to doctrinal statements. Remember, the devils also believe and tremble. Before you accuse me of believing in salvation through works, I assure you that I believe we are saved by grace through faith.

But now I need to tell you what I think these two words, grace and faith, mean in the context of Christianity and then to consider some scriptures to see if my use of them is Biblical. Grace is the unmerited love and favor of God toward man which includes the gift of eternal life and the power to live a life of obedience to God and characterized by the fruit of the Spirit. Faith is an intellectual assent to the doctrinal teachings of Christianity and a radical and total commitment to Christ as Lord of one's life, an abandonment of trust in oneself, a reliance on Christ for salvation, a reliance on the power of the Spirit for strength, and a reliance on and obedience to God.

Why is it so easy for us to believe that God will give us health or wealth, but have no faith at all that He is able to empower us to live a godly life? We believe that when we ask anything in His will, He will grant it. We do not know that it is His will that we should become wealthy. In fact, we are warned over and over that wealth is a very dangerous thing and that Jesus told at least one man to give away everything he had. Even health is not known to be God's will for everyone in every circumstance. The great apostle Paul found that out. On the other hand, the New Testament makes it abundantly clear that an obedient life is God's will for us. Then why can't we pray, in faith, that He will enable us to live that life?

Romans 4 is often cited as the basis for a "faith only" salvation. Paul gives Abraham as an example of a man who was justified by faith not works. However, James says that Abraham was justified by what he did and not by faith alone. If one doesn't read the rest of what James (and Paul) said, this sounds contradictory. But, James said that Abraham's faith and actions were working together and that his faith was made complete by what he did. I think that James was fighting the belief in a magical incantation. This kind of a belief in magic is really a mirage, and it was and is an incorrect interpretation of Paul's teaching.

In Romans 4, Paul is rightly emphasizing that there are no works that we can do to merit salvation. It is only through faith, a radical commitment to Christ as Lord of one's life, that God's grace saves us. But when we put our trust in God, then His grace empowers us to obey

Him. Do you honestly believe that Abraham would have been cited for his great faith if he had not followed any of God's commands? Imagine Abraham hearing God's call to journey to a far land and saying, "Oh Lord, I hear and I have faith in You. Now I am going to stay right here in my tent because I know that I am justified by faith and not by works." Similarly, it does not make sense to say "Father, I believe that you are an all powerful, all loving God, without You I can do nothing but make my life miserable. Now go away and don't come back until I die and then take me home to heaven."

This is such a travesty of Paul's teaching! Please reread Romans 4 carefully and then chapters 5 and 6, especially 6. In chapter 5, he says that since we have been justified by faith, we have access to grace and that grace reigns through righteousness. In chapter 6, he emphasizes over and over that we have died to sin, we are free from sin. "For sin shall not be your master, because you are not under law, but under grace" (v. 14). "You have been set free from sin and have become slaves to righteousness" (v. 18). And then verse 22 states it so clearly: "But now you have been set free from sin and have become slaves to God, the benefit you reap leads to holiness, and the result is eternal life."

In Ephesians 2:8-10, Paul says, "For by grace you have been saved through faith; and this is not your own doing, it is the gift of God not because of works, lest any man should boast. For we are his workmanship, created in Christ Jesus for good works, which God prepared beforehand, that we should walk in them." Now if God has prepared good works for me to do and I have faith in God, can I then refuse to do the good works? James makes it even clearer. "What does it profit, my brethren, if a man says he has faith but has not works? Can his faith save him? If a brother or sister is ill clad and in lack of daily food, and one of you says to them 'Go in peace, be warmed and filled,' without giving them the things needed for the body, what does it profit? So faith by itself, if it has no works, is dead" (James 1:14-17). Faith, if it does not lead to love and obedience is dead. Jesus said, "Truly, truly, I say to you, if anyone keeps my word, he will never see death" (John 8:51). That is, obedience leads to eternal life. But we know that faith leads to eternal life. So how can we have faith without obedience?

Sometimes the concept of "imputed righteousness" is taught as though God looks at our moral filthiness and calls it purity, or like a father throwing a clean robe over the dirty and diseased body of a child so he wouldn't need to look at it or touch it. A loving father would try to clean and heal the child with his own hands. Surely we would not be satisfied when we pray for someone suffering from cancer if God's answer would be, "It's alright, I will look upon the person as if he did not have cancer." The grace of our loving Heavenly Father is willing to take us, dirty as we are, into His arms and begin the purifying process.

Jesus used the term "born again" for salvation. This was a metaphor, but an apt metaphor means something. Nicodemus recognized that this was a radical metaphor. It signifies a great change. Being born is the greatest, most abrupt change we ever made. Think of it, going from your mother's womb into the outside world, from receiving literally everything from your mother to being on your own. Certainly, everyone can see the difference between "before and after." Why would Jesus use such a radical metaphor? He must have wanted us to see the radical change He had in store for us. Can you imagine a baby in the womb just before birth saying, "Yes, I have faith. I want to be born, but if you don't mind, I'll just stay in here where it's so comfortable." Impossible, of course, but is it any different from a person saying, "Yes, I have faith. I want to be born again, but if you don't mind, I'll just stay as I am because it's so comfortable."

Some people who understand the importance of works think that an overemphasis on grace tends to keep people from doing good works. This is not true. I don't think that we can overemphasize grace. It is only by God's grace that we can live a Christian life. But by God's grace it can be done.

Why do you suppose that so many believe in a grace that saves but does not sanctify? I think it is because that is what we want to believe. We want to be safe but free to do whatever we want to do. In an old Christian devotional classic, *A Serious Call to a Devout and Holy Life*, William Law says that if we will stop and ask ourselves why we are not as pious as we should be, our hearts will tell us that it is neither through ignorance nor inability but purely because we never thoroughly intended it.[1] If we only had the serious intent to be what we should be, then God's grace could begin to work in our lives. We often plead with God to use us, but He can't use us until we are fit to use. We should plead with Him to clean us up, put a new heart within us and then we will be used without asking.

It may sound as if I am saying that unless a person is perfect, he or she is not a Christian and that I have achieved this perfectly obedient life. This is far from the truth. I do not claim to be perfectly obeying God and certainly am not judging anyone. I am only trusting in God's grace to enable me to follow Him nearer and nearer as time goes by. This miracle that God works in our lives is a process, not a magical instantaneous transformation. II Cor. 3:18 says that "we, who with unveiled faces all reflect the Lord's glory, are being transformed into his likeness with ever-increasing glory which comes from the Lord, who is the Spirit."

We cannot judge one another because only God knows where we have come from, where we are, and where we are headed. George MacDonald has said that God is easy to please but hard to satisfy. It is just like a mother who sees her son take his first step. She is very pleased, but certainly would not be satisfied if her son would go through life walking no better than on that day he took his first step.

As any of you who have looked through a telescope know there are beautiful galaxies in the sky. Someone who believes in salvation by works would be like an astronomer who tries to draw with his own hand a picture of the galaxy. Someone who believes in a magical faith only would be like an astronomer who wants a picture but does not bother to place the film where the image will hit it or point the telescope at the galaxy. One who understands what Paul and James were saying is like the astronomer who carefully places the film in the right place, points the telescope at the galaxy, and then continues to turn the telescope so that it stays on the galaxy, not because the galaxy is moving but because the earth is. The result then is that the light itself makes an accurate, and hence beautiful picture of the galaxy.

The importance of all this is shown by the following quotation from William Barclay.

> "Long ago Nietzsche, the German atheist philosopher said: 'Show me that you are redeemed, and I will believe in your redeemer.' Justification, like grace, brings a man an immense privilege and lays on a man an immense responsibility. Judgment is an essential part of the Christian faith for the very simple reason that Christianity is meant to make a man a certain kind of man, and enables him to be that kind of man; and, if he fails to be that kind of man, then there is only one conclusion—he is not really Christian; and the fault is his, for the enabling grace was there."[2]

It is important to resist what is, from a human standpoint, an attractive belief in magic, but which is only a mirage; and to be open to the miraculous grace of God, which is ready, willing, and able to begin, continue, and complete the process of transforming us into His likeness with ever increasing splendor.

Changed Lives

"Christian morality is the most beautiful thing on our planet.
When you see it—really see it—the quest is over."

E. Stanley Jones

The basic outline and idea for this chapter comes from a sermon by Henry Drummond entitled "The Changed Life." The thesis of the sermon is that if even just a few of us would show truly transformed Christian lives, it would have a tremendous effect on the world. Remember that in Jesus' prayer recorded in John 17, He prayed that we might have the loving unity that He and the Father have with each other and that if we did, then the world would know that Jesus is from God and that God loves them. Jesus also said, "By this shall all men know that you are my disciples, if you have love for one another" (John 13:35).

This change that Jesus expects of us is a very drastic one. He said that our love must show in ways beyond what is considered natural, beyond what tax collectors do (Matt. 5:38-47). He even said, "You, therefore, must be perfect, as your heavenly Father is perfect." What does this mean, and how could this kind of change come about?

This kind of change seems so strange, even unnatural, probably even impossible except for very rare, impractical people, people out of touch with reality. Besides, does it really matter? After all, God knows we can't really attain perfect love. I think the New Testament teaches that it is really important. It has a real effect on our Christian witness. So often our witness is like a five foot, 300 pound man who says, "Use Brand X reducing pills. I do and they really work."

Since it is so important, why aren't changed lives more evident? Don't people really want to change? I think many would like to change. However, few "hunger and thirst after righteousness" the way we must, if we are to be filled. Many have tried to be better and have failed. Thus, they have become discouraged and believe it is impossible to change. There is no way we can change by our own strength.

Drummond compares this kind of effort with a man trying to move a sailboat by standing on the deck and pushing against the mast.

There are passages in the Bible that seem to indicate that the changed life is a gift rather than a result of our own efforts. Galatians 5:22 lists goodness as a fruit of the Spirit. An apple tree doesn't try to grow apples. Apples just grow on it. Romans 12:2 says, "Let your minds be remade and your whole nature thus transformed." The passive form is used. Something is being done to us. It is not something we are doing.

Therefore, all we need to do is pray to God for help, and He will change us! But most of us have prayed for God's help and still keep on sinning. It doesn't seem to work. We try to change and nothing happens. We pray and nothing happens. Maybe it's the combination. We need to keep both trying to be good and asking God to make us good. We really do need to do both of those things, but even then it usually does not seem to work well. By this time in the process, most people have given up and decided that we can't make very significant progress towards perfection in this life.

Let's consider again the command to be perfect. One interpretation is that it was given to show that what God requires is impossible, but He will accept us anyway. There is some truth in this. He will accept us just as we are, but He is ready to begin the process "for building up the body of Christ, until we all attain to the unity of the faith and of the knowledge of the Son of God, to mature manhood, to the measure of the stature of the fullness of Christ" (Eph. 4:12b-13). So it is a process, not an instantaneous transformation and, as the passage in the first part of Ephesians 4 indicates, the church or body of believers is a part of that process.

If we think of perfection as only an ideal, we become too easily satisfied with what we are. There is too much evidence in the New Testament that God expects us to change. C. S. Lewis has some helpful comments on this. He thinks that God was saying, "The only help I will give is help to become perfect. You may want something less: but I will give you nothing less."[1] He goes on to say that so often we ask God for help only in certain areas, areas where we would like to change, but want God to ignore areas where we need change but don't want to. Lewis illustrates this with an incident from his childhood. As a little boy, he often had toothache. Sometimes he couldn't sleep because of the pain. He knew that he could go to his mother, and she would give him something to kill the pain and let him go to sleep. Yet he would not go to his mother for help unless the pain was very bad because he knew that if he did, then in the morning she would make an appointment with the dentist. That was before the days of "painless" dentists. And they would not only take care of the aching tooth but also would start "fiddling about with all sorts of other teeth which had not yet begun to ache. They would not let sleeping dogs lie; if you gave them an inch they took an ell."[2] We can't go to God and say, "Here is one part of my life causing me pain. Help it, but don't meddle anywhere else." No, our first duty, the first and perhaps the biggest step towards a changed life, is to be willing to say to God, "Here I am, go to work where and how You will." Then God can begin the process, but I believe we still have a part to play also.

To become Christlike, we must know Christ. Learning more about Christ is a step on the way to becoming like Him. This is a natural phenomenon. Think of a person you know well, love, and spend much time with. You are becoming like that person. With different friends we act differently. Haven't you noticed similarities in people who have been married to each other for thirty or forty years? I think that usually a husband and wife who have lived together and loved each other for a long time are more alike than natural brother and sister.

So we must get to know Jesus of Nazareth. But how is it possible to know someone who lived 2,000 years ago? Again, even on a natural level, we can know people who lived a long time ago. One of my hobbies is reading about Abraham Lincoln. I have read well over a hundred books about his life and times including his collected works. Not everything written in the books is true, yet by comparing and thinking and discussing him with others one can get at the truth of Abraham

Lincoln. I know him better than any present day leader, better than I know many of my neighbors and colleagues. It is possible to know someone who lived long ago. And in the process, we might become a little more like him or her.

In the same way that I got to know Lincoln, I can get to know Christ. However, there are also supernatural forces that help us to know Him. First, instead of fallible biographies written by men and women, we have the inspired word of God. "All scripture is inspired by God and is profitable for reproof, for correction, and for training in righteousness, that the man of God may be complete, equipped for every good work" (II Tim. 3:16-17). Second, we have a divine helper. "When the Spirit of truth comes, he will guide you into all the truth; for he will not speak on his own authority, but whatever he hears he will speak, and he will declare to you the things that are to come. He will glorify me, for he will take what is mine and declare it to you" (John 16:13-14). Third, Ephesians 4:11-16 tells us that individuals in the church are given various gifts to enable us to grow to "the measure of the stature of the fullness of Christ."

Jesus invites us to come and learn from Him (Matt. 11:28-29). Peter tells us to "grow in the grace and knowledge of our Lord and Savior Jesus Christ" (II Peter 3:18). John says that "we shall be like him, for we shall see him as he is" (I John 3:2). This latter verse probably does not refer to this life, but the more clearly we see Him now, the more nearly will we be like Him.

Perhaps the best description of this process of change is found in II Corinthians 3:18. "And because for us there is no veil over the face, we all reflect as in a mirror the splendor of the Lord; thus we are transfigured into His likeness, from splendor to splendor; such is the influence of the Lord who is Spirit" (NEB). We must imitate Christ in whatever ways we can. That is how obedience to what we know, however little, leads to greater knowledge and greater likeness to Christ. The analogy of the mirror gives us insight into another aspect. A mirror doesn't try to look like something else; it simply reflects whatever is in front of it. When we face Christ, His image will be reflected from us and, the verse goes on to say, we will continually be changing from splendor to splendor.

Consider again the analogy of the astronomer and telescope of the last chapter. Certainly we must try to do what is right, and we must pray for the Spirit to help us. However, perhaps our greatest effort should be made to keep our focus on Jesus, remembering that in this changing world it takes constant work to keep an unchanging point in focus. As we focus on Christ, we reflect his glory, and the Spirit works in us, transfiguring us into His likeness Then, and only then, I believe, will people see a love so glorious that they will know here is something so wonderful that they must have it too.

Successful Superstar or Suffering Servant

"The prevailing attitudes of the culture have thoroughly infiltrated the ranks of faith and belief."

Charles Colson

Who would you most want to be like ten years from now? Bill Gates, Bobby Knight, Einstein, Gandhi, Michael Jackson, Jesse Jackson, Marilyn Monroe, or Mother Teresa? The values we hold, the basic beliefs we have, are determining the kind of persons we are becoming. I don't mean what we say we believe in church or even what we tell ourselves we believe, but rather the values we actually live by. Just as in mathematics the axioms determine the theorems, so my basic beliefs determine the type of person I will be.

The axioms of this world are not the same as the axioms of the Kingdom of God. Paul said, "Adapt yourselves no longer to the pattern of this present world, but let your minds be remade and your whole nature thus transformed. Then you will be able to discern the will of God, and to know what is good, acceptable, and perfect" (Romans 12:2, NEB).

Thomas Jefferson was a revolutionary. He said, "We hold these truths to be self-evident…" He went on to state his axioms and show that they led to a radical change in the government, from a monarchy in England to a democracy in North America. Jesus was even more of a revolutionary. He said, "I hold these truths, whether they are self-evident to you or not. People are happy when they know they are poor, when they are gentle, hungry and thirsty to see right prevail, merciful, pure in heart, peacemakers, and even when they suffer persecution and insults for the cause of goodness". These are the axioms or the constitution of the Kingdom of God. They certainly are not the world's axioms. Our problem is that we are citizens of God's Kingdom while physically residing in an alien culture, one that is ruled, however subtly, by Satan, the prince of the power of the air, the ruler of the darkness of this world.

This world's values are constantly bombarding us. We breathe in the poisoned culture just like polluted air. The world's axioms are in much of what we read, watch and listen to. On television we see no warning from the Surgeon General of the United States or the Executive Secretary of the National Association of Evangelicals that "the following program may be detrimental to your spiritual health." The basic beliefs underlying popular culture are not stated, only implied. If they were stated explicitly, we would recognize that they are non-Christian. TV programs and movies depict lives determined by the world's values and imply that all normal people live the same way.

If we are citizens of God's Kingdom, then we must live by those laws, even though we are presently living in an alien country. Consider an American citizen living in China (or vice versa). There are many things which would be appropriate for a Chinese citizen to do in China which would be utterly inappropriate for an American citizen in the same situation. Where one's citizenship resides is important.

The world's values have even infiltrated the church, not Communism or secular humanism but simply secularization. We give lip service to God, but live by what we call practical, and what we call practical is determined by the secular beliefs. For example, in business the world considers looking out for one's self more important than being concerned about our customers; or in politics, a little white lie or even a misleading statement might be "necessary" to achieve a good goal. If the axioms that Jesus stated are true, then what the world calls practical is very impractical, indeed. George MacDonald said, "Because a man would live according to the laws of his being as well as his body, obeying simple, imperative, essential human necessity, his fellows forsooth call him <u>impractical</u>! Of the idiotic delusions of the children of this world, that of being practical is one of the most ludicrous."[1]

The Sermon on the Mount is often twisted to make it fit the world's axioms. It seems strange and impractical, so we spiritualize it or say it is for another dispensation, and ignore the parable at the end of the sermon, which says that those who hear and obey are like a wise man who built his house upon the rock. It doesn't seem right to us because the world has captured our minds, we have become conformed, we have allowed the world to squeeze us into its mold. We need to have our minds renewed. A brain transplant is what we need! Or, as Juan Carlos Ortiz wrote, "We must let God take out our brains, wash them in detergent, brush them, and put them back in the other way. Our whole set of values must be changed."[2]   Ortiz goes on to compare us to medieval people who believed everything revolved around the earth. They were wrong, and so are we when we believe that we are the center and everything is for our personal enjoyment. God is the center, not us.

A model of the Christian life that seems to be prevalent in today's church is that of the successful superstar. According to this teaching, the purpose of Christianity is to change us from mediocrities to stars. Here is a hypothetical example of what I mean. A baseball player says, "I was hitting .185 and was very depressed. I was about to be sent down to the minors or released altogether when I asked Jesus into my heart. Now I am hitting .365, have hit 45 home runs, won the golden glove award, and have just signed a multimillion dollar five year contract." Of course, I have exaggerated, but unfortunately, not very much.

Instead of "successful superstar," the authentic Christian model is "suffering servant." Jesus Christ is our model, and Isaiah described him as "a man of sorrows, and acquainted with grief" (Isaiah 53:3). Paul said, "Your attitude should be the same as that of Christ Jesus: Who being in very nature God, did not consider equality with God something to be grasped, but made himself nothing, taking the very nature of a servant, being made in human likeness. And being found in appearance as a man, he humbled himself and became obedient to death—even death on a cross" (Phil. 2:5-8, NIV). Jesus said, "I am among you as one who serves (Luke 22:27). Peter said of suffering, "To this you were called, because Christ suffered for you leaving you an example, that you should follow in His steps" (I Peter 2:21, NIV).

It is sad that Christians and non-Christians alike are getting the message from many church leaders and TV evangelists that the "successful superstar" and not the "suffering servant" is the Christian model. It is sad because it is not true and is thus a great hindrance to the growth of the Kingdom of God. And it is sad because of the paradox that the "successful superstar" model eventually leads to boredom, depression, and despair while the "suffering servant" model leads to true joy.

Who experiences the most joy and true happiness and contentment, a movie or rock music star making millions of dollars or Mother Teresa? Many movie and rock stars have turned to drugs and even suicide because their lives are so meaningless and miserable. "Those who have seen Mother Teresa and her Sisters working in a leprosarium all testify that they are joyous and would not think of giving up this work."[3] Mother Teresa said to her Sisters, her coworkers, "Suffering in itself is nothing, but suffering that shares in the Passion of Christ is a wonderful gift and a sign of love. How good God is to give you so much suffering and so much love. All of this is joy to me and gives me strength on account of you. It is your life of sacrifice that gives me strength."[4] She also said, "This is the true reason for our existence, to be the sunshine of God's love, to be the hope of eternal happiness. That's all."[5]

Peter refers to the paradox in these words, "Dear friends, do not be surprised at the painful trial you are suffering, as though something strange were happening to you. But rejoice that you participate in the suffering of Christ, so that you may be overjoyed when his glory is revealed" (I Peter 4:12-13, NIV). Paul's testimony was, "We know sorrow, yet our joy is inextinguishable. We have 'nothing to bless ourselves with,' yet we bless many others with true riches. We are penniless, and yet in reality we have everything worth having" (II Cor. 6:10, Phillips).

Even though the "suffering servant" is our model, it does not mean that we should go through life seeking pain, but we must seek ways of serving others. Suffering will come in whatever ways God sees fit. But whatever comes, the Holy Spirit will give us joy in this life and the hope of eternal joy in the life to come.

Compare the World's and the Kingdom's axioms in the following paragraphs. Consider how the Kingdom axioms lead to suffering but joyous servanthood.

The world advises, "Do your own thing." Songs proclaim, "I'll do it my way." The poet says, "I am the master of my fate, I am the captain of my soul." The Kingdom says that we must surrender our will and obey God We are not our own masters: Jesus is Lord. We are told to pray, "Thy kingdom come, Thy will be done" (Matt. 6:10). Jesus said, "If you love me, you will keep my commandments" (John 14:15).

The world says that we must have pride in ourselves. As the lady in a TV commercial says, "It's expensive, but I'm worth it." In the Kingdom we must realize that we are poor and needy and we are to think about others instead of ourselves. "Blessed are the poor in spirit...the meek" (Matt. 5:3,5). "Do nothing out of selfish ambition or vain conceit, but in humility consider others better than yourselves" (Phil. 2:3, NIV).

The world assumes that we should avoid pain and sorrow as much as possible and that death is a terrible tragedy. On the other hand we must seek happiness and "grab all the gusto we can, since we only go around once." However, we have already seen that it is good to know sorrow (Matt. 5:4), and even death need not be feared. "Whether we live or whether we die, we are the Lord's" (Rom. 14:8). Paul said, "For me to live is Christ, and to die is gain." (Phil. 1:21).

One of the main axioms of our society is the idea that money brings joy and security. Our whole economy is based on consumerism. Almost every TV commercial implies that things bring us happiness. However, the Kingdom axiom is clear: we can't depend on material things. It is God who takes care of us. "Do not lay up for yourselves treasures on earth, where moth and rust consume and where thieves break in and steal,but lay up for yourselves tresures in heaven, where neither moth nor rust consumes and where thieves do not break in and steal." (Matt. 6:19-20, KJV). "But if God so clothes the grass of the field which today is alive and tomorrow is thrown into the oven, will he not much more clothe you, O men of little faith?" (Matt. 6:30). "Are not five sparrows sold for two pennies? Yet not one of them is forgotten by

God. Indeed the very hairs of your head are all numbered. Don't be afraid: you are worth more than many sparrows" (Luke 12:6-7, NIV). We are warned about the deceitfulness of wealth in Matthew 13:22, also in Matthew 19:16-20, Luke 12:33, and I Timothy 6:5-11.

The world tells us that we must look after number one. If I don't take care of myself, who will? Again the Kingdom axiom is the opposite: I am responsible for and must serve others. The importance of our responsibility is given in Matthew 18:6: "Whoever causes one of these little ones who believe in me to sin, it would be better for him to have a great millstone fastened round his neck and to be drowned in the depths of the sea." In the parable of the sheep and goats (Matt. 25:31-46), we are told to feed the hungry, clothe the naked, welcome the strangers, and visit those who are sick or in prison.

We need to study the Bible to become more familiar with the constitution of the Kingdom of God. We need to examine our culture to determine which of its axioms are contrary to the Kingdom's axioms and how culture attempts to indoctrinate us. Our aim should be to live a consistent life as a citizen of God's Kingdom. God promised us help to do this. "I will sprinkle clean water on you, and you will be clean; I will cleanse you from all your impurities and from your idols. I will give you a new heart and put a new spirit in you; I will remove from you your heart of stone and give you a heart of flesh. And I will put my Spirit in you and move you to follow my decrees and be careful to obey my laws" (Ezekiel 36:25-28).

Then we must remember that the only path to real joy is obedience to God's laws. As the poet Nath Tagore said,
"I slept and I dreamed
that life is all joy.
I woke and I saw
that life is all service.
I served and I saw
that service is joy!"[6]

The Simple Life

"Purity of heart is to will one thing."
Soren Kierkegaard

Dr. Paul Brand tells of a beggar woman he saw in Madras, India. "Like many Indian beggars, the woman was emaciated, with sunken cheeks and eyes and bony limbs. But, paradoxically, a huge mass of plump skin, round and sleek like a sausage, was growing from her side. It lay beside her like a formless baby, connected to her by a broad bridge of skin. The woman had exposed her flank with its grotesque deformity to give her an advantage in the rivalry for pity."[1]

Dr. Brand says that the growth was a lipoma, a benign tumor of fat cells. He goes on to describe the good purposes of fat cells: insulation against cold, cushions vital body parts, physical appearance, and storage of fuel. The fatty tumor develops when a fat cell rebels and instead of giving up its store of fat when the body needs it, hoards it and produces more fat cells that do the same. In other words, the cells in the lipoma were thriving at the expense of the cells in the rest of the body, which were slowly starving to death.

This seemed to Dr. Brand to be an image of the Christian church. He said, "At Vellore we treated leprosy patients on three dollars per patient per year; yet we turned many away for lack of funds. Then we came to America where churches were heatedly discussing their million-dollar gymnasiums and the cost of landscaping and fertilizer and a new steeple…and sponsoring seminars on tax shelters for members to conserve their accumulated wealth."[2] That is, some cells in the body of Christ have mutinied and are not using their wealth in legitimate ways for the good of the entire body but are hoarding them for their own selfish uses.

Is this an apt analogy? Most of us Christians in the United States do not consider ourselves wealthy. But that is because we compare ourselves to those around us instead of to people in the rest of the world. The statistics cited in the next few paragraphs describes the conditions about twenty-five years ago. However, the situation, in all likelihood, is just as bad or worse today. In the U.S.A. we consume nearly three times as much cereal per capita as does Japan and nearly five times as much as developing countries.[3] It is probably worse for meat, sugar, or soft drinks. In spite of eating so much more, we only spend 17% of our disposable income on food compared to 23% in Japan, 52% in Peru, 62% in Zaire, and 67% in India. It is even worse in energy consumption. We use 342 times as much energy per capita as Ethiopia, 64 times as much as India, and 21 times as much as Brazil.

The United States, "containing only 5.6% of the world's population, has been consuming 42% of the world's output of aluminum, 33% of its copper, 44% of the world's coal, 33% of its petroleum and 63% of its natural gas."[4] In general, it takes "forty percent of the world's primary resources to supply less than six percent of the world's population."[5] "Even on the conservative side about half a billion—that's 500 million!—people in the world are gradually starving, receiving less than the baseline requirement of calories. Another half billion get enough calories but are short on protein."[6] It is pretty evident that in the United States we are using much more than our share of the world's resources.

There is no doubt in my mind that we ought to live more frugally and use the money we save to help the poor. However, there are still two (at least) problems. One is that it is so hard to use money wisely. Often the poor are hurt more than helped by attempts to use money to solve their problems. More about that later in the chapter. The other problem is that as a motivation to live a simple life living frugally, even to help the poor, just isn't very effective for many people. Tolstoy found this out over a century ago. The reply to his appeal to his rich friends to live more simply so that they could help the needy was, "Even if I wear dirty linen and stop smoking and give this money to the poor instead, all the same the poor will have everything taken from them, and my drop in the ocean will not help matters."[7] Tolstoy's answer is that that is probably true. However, he went on to say that if he were

living among cannibals, it would probably not help the people sched-
uled to be on the menu if he would refuse to eat them. Still, he <u>would</u>
refuse.

Therefore, although the problem of extreme poverty in the world
shows the need for a simpler life style, desire to help the needy usually
doesn't provide adequate motivation. We get discouraged and say, as
Tolstoy's friends said, "My little bit doesn't really do much good."
Perhaps the ecological problem would provide adequate motivation.
The excessive use of wood, coal, and oil for fuel is increasing the level
of carbon dioxide in the air, as is the destruction of vast areas of rain
forest for short term benefits. This increased level of carbon dioxide
has a greenhouse effect on the whole planet, which could have disastrous results. Acid rain, air pollution, water pollution, soil pollution
(due to high level use of commercial fertilizers) and other potential
disasters are all in the offing. It may be a close race as to which will
destroy our society. Besides this, within a hundred years most of the
non-renewable resources, which are so important to our lifestyles, will
be nearly depleted. However, as motivation for living a more simple
life, this suffers from the same difficulty as before. My little bit won't
solve the problem, so I might just as well enjoy life while I can.

Enjoyment is a great motivator. Isn't the simple life more fun?
Maybe here we have found sufficient motivation. After all, as
Schumacher has pointed out, modern economists are wrong in "as-
suming all the time that a man who consumes more is 'better off' than
a man who consumes less."[8] Instead, our "aim should be to obtain the
maximum of well-being with the minimum of consumption."[9] As Isaiah
asked long ago, "Why spend money on what is not bread, and your
labor on what does not satisfy?" (Isaiah 55:2, NIV)

I believe that most of us could greatly simplify our lives, and in the
long run, by doing so we would be much happier. The catch is "in the
long run." There are many things that would not be enjoyable at first.
Parenthetically, some parts might never be, but the whole would eventually be better. It is like someone who is addicted to cigarettes or

drugs. Eventually, I believe, the person would be happier without them, but at first would be miserable. We are addicted to consumerism and would suffer withdrawal symptoms if we tried to stop. Therefore, hedonism is not adequate to motivate us to live as we should.

In an excellent book, The Simple Life, Vernard Eller points out the problems with these and other motivations. Then he shows us the only motivation capable of enabling us to live the simple life. It is found in the Sermon on the Mount. Jesus said, "No one can serve two masters. Either he will hate the one and love the other, or he will be devoted to one and despise the other. You cannot serve both God and Money" (Matt. 6:24, NIV). Many Christians are unhappy because they have divided loyalties. The world's culture has seduced them into serving money or other gods while they are still trying to serve God. That is what complicates life. To simplify our lives we need a single aim.

Jesus also said, "Seek first his kingdom and his righteousness, and all these things shall be yours as well" (Matt. 6:33). It sounds as if He is telling us to put two things, his kingdom and his righteousness, in first place. If so, that would really complicate things. Actually, there aren't two things here. His righteousness and his kingdom are exactly the same. The only adequate motivation to live a simple life is to seek first God's kingdom and righteousness.

Eller then quotes Kierkegaard,

What does this mean, what have I to do, or what sort of effort is it that can be said to seek or pursue the kingdom of God? Shall I try to get a job suitable to my talents and powers in order thereby to exert an influence? No, thou shalt first seek God's kingdom. Shall I then give all my fortune to the poor? No, thou shalt first seek God's kingdom. Shall I then go out to proclaim this teaching to the world? No, thou shalt first seek God's kingdom. But then in a certain sense it is nothing I shall do. Yes, certainly in a certain sense it is nothing; thou shalt in the deepest sense make thyself nothing, become nothing before God, learn to keep silent; in this silence is the beginning, which is first to seek God's kingdom.[10]

We might need to do some or all of those things mentioned by Kierkegaard but not <u>first</u>. Eller says,

> "It is incredible that a person could freely and wholeheartedly choose God and become absolutely obedient to him without it making some change in his relationship to things of this world. If some sort of outward change did not take place, it rightly could be suspected whether he had actually chosen God. That change, of course will be in the direction of simplicity, a lessened evaluation of what the world promotes as important."[11]

Kierkegaard has an interesting parable about possessions.[12]   Remember that Kierkegaard lived in the first half of the nineteenth century. When a rich man travels in his carriage at night, he has plenty of lanterns so he can see where he is going. With lots of light he can travel safely. However, because of these bright lights, he cannot see the stars. A peasant driving without lights can enjoy the beautiful starry sky. So it is with us. With many possessions, we feel comfortable and secure, but they obscure the vision of the heavens. Now if we rid ourselves of some of these possessions in order to see God more clearly, we will have more to share with the needy and will not be polluting our environment so much. But the most important thing is to seek God's kingdom first of all and the rest will fall into place.

Churches as well as individuals need to get their priorities straight. In 1976, Eastminster Presbyterian Church in Wichita, Kansas was planning a $525,000 building program. When an earthquake destroyed thousands of homes, churches, and other buildings in Guatemala, a lay person in the church posed the question, "How can we…buy an ecclesiastical Cadillac when our brothers and sisters in Guatemala have just lost their little Volkswagen?"[13] So plans were changed. They opted for a $180,000 building program and after visiting Christians in Guatemala, borrowed $120,000 to rebuild twenty-six Guatemalan churches and twenty-six Guatemalan pastors' houses. They are continuing to help their fellow Christians in Central America, and the church is growing spiritually and numerically.

The fact that the church is growing numerically is important to note. People often say that they must spend lots of money in order to have a nice building so that people will be attracted to their church. I'm afraid that people who are attracted by a building may not really be entering the Kingdom of God and that some others may be put off if they see Christians spending valuable resources on a building when there are so many needs in the world. After all, the early church experienced a fantastic growth without any buildings at all.

Once we are earnestly seeking God's kingdom and His righteousness and have thus simplified our lives, we are freed to proclaim and live out the gospel in a way that brings good news to the poor and liberty to the oppressed. John Perkins has a strategy he calls the "Three R's." They are relocation, reconciliation, and redistribution.

Redistribution of resources is more feasible once we realize we don't need so many things. But money is not the only, or even the most important, thing that needs to be redistributed. The poor need our talents and time also. Christians themselves need to be redistributed. This brings us to the R of relocation.

In order to really help people, we need to live in the same community with them so that we can experience their problems first hand and identify with them. My son was working with the poor in a favela (slum) in Recife, Brazil. At first he lived outside the favela in a nice neighborhood and went to the favela each day. Things were just not going well until he moved into a shack in the favela and lived with them. Perkins says that people who try to help from the outside develop a "welfare mentality" and come up with programs that often retard and dehumanize those they are supposed to help. Mother Teresa said, "We do not want to do what other religious orders have done throughout history, and begin by serving the poor only to end up unconsciously serving the rich. In order to understand and help those who have nothing, we must live like them."[14] When God wanted to help us, He didn't get on TV from heaven with the message for us. He relocated. That is the meaning of the incarnation.

The third R is reconciliation. As long as we are using more than our share of the world's resources as the statistics in the early part of this chapter indicated, it is difficult to imagine how reconciliation can take place. The most important reconciliation is that of man or woman to God. But how can that take place when God's representatives are living in ways that cause severe injustices?

John Perkins said, "A gospel that doesn't reconcile is not a Christian gospel at all. But in America it seems as if we don't believe that. We don't really believe that the proof of our discipleship is that we love one another (See John 13:35). No, we think the proof is in numbers—church attendance, decision cards. Even if our 'converts' continue to hate each other, even if they will not worship with their brothers and sisters in Christ, we point to their 'conversion' as evidence of the gospel's success. We have substituted a gospel of church growth for a gospel of reconciliation."[15]

The simple life can only be achieved by placing God first. Then we are freed to evangelize and also freed to enjoy life. Paradoxically, it turns out that in a sense hedonism is the motive behind Christian simplicity. Living simply for the sake of living simply may not be enjoyable, but living simply for the sake of God and his kingdom is. This point is made also in Eller's book, *The Simple Life*. By the way, I think that his book is the best of the many that I have read on that subject. Therefore, it seems appropriate to close this chapter with one more quote from his book.

> Christian simplicity is so to use "things" that, first, they do not interfere with one's absolute joy in God, and second, they actually point toward and contribute to that joy. When "things" are given their proper evaluation as being creations of and gifts from the God who loves us and supplies us with every good, then they can operate as integral contributions to that joy.[16]

Community

"It is not customary that an intelligent person clothes and cares for one part of his body and leaves the rest naked. The intelligent person is solicitous for all his members. Thus it should be with those who are the Lord's church and body and are prepared by love to serve their neighbors."

Menno Simons, 1552

Mathematics teaches us that we must have a starting point. Since it is not possible to prove every statement, we must start with some assumptions. We could give reasons for the statements that we assume, but then other statements would have to be accepted. Also, for a mathematician the words axiom, postulate, and assumption are synonymous.

In this chapter, we will explore some of the implications of basic Christian beliefs on community. I am starting with Christian axioms because those are my beliefs. This does not mean that non-Christians will necessarily disagree with my conclusions. The basic axioms I use may be equivalent to those of many who are not Christians or the conclusions may be accepted for other reasons. But I have to start where I am.

The method of mathematics is to formulate the basic propositions (axioms) needed for whatever study is under consideration and then to prove all the theorems one can. Obviously, this chapter will not be a complete mathematical structure. However, I do believe it is important for each of us to be aware of our basic beliefs and whether our daily actions are logically consistent with those beliefs. Many of our problems today, individually and as a society, are due to inconsistencies between various parts of our lives. In spite of our valiant attempts to compartmentalize, I don't believe that it can be done by a thinking person without repression and resulting stress of various kinds.

My first axiom is that God is love. Another is that all of His creation in some way reflects His character, and in particular, people are created in His image. Therefore, since God is love, love is at the heart of the creation. Since an isolated individual cannot experience love, community is essential. Man's well-being and happiness come through community, not isolation.

Another axiom is that the Bible is God's word. From the Old Testament's, "Behold, how good and how pleasant it is for brethren to dwell together in unity" (Psalms 133:1), to the New Testament's "Bear ye one another's burdens, and so fulfill the law of Christ" (Gal. 6:2), the Bible clearly teaches the importance of community. One of its most striking metaphors for the church is that of a body.

Our society stresses competition more than compassion and that works against community. In fact, it seems that, for most of us, competition is our main motivation in life. Certainly, athletics emphasizes competition. At times our community newspaper features a local athlete. One of the questions each athlete is asked is, "Why do you like baseball (or basketball, etc.)?" Usually the answer is, "I enjoy the competition." Only rarely does someone say, "It is a team sport and everyone has to do his part." Our culture could stress cooperation, but competition usully prevails.

In education also, competition with others is often used as the main motivation. In our jobs and in our recreation, we evaluate ourselves by comparison with others. As Henri Nouwen and his coauthors point out,

> "We define ourselves in ways that require us to maintain distance from one another. We are very protective of our 'trophies.' After all, who are we if we cannot proudly point to something special that sets us apart from others? This all pervasive competition...stands in the way of our being compassionate."[1]

Our fallen nature and the encouragement of cultural forces make competition the primary motivation for so many of us. Remember, however, that love or compassion, is basic to our true natures.

The fact that our Western society is so interdependent, probably more so than any other society of the present, or past, would seem to support community, but there are problems. Our dependence is on people who are remote, people we do not know, instead of on our neighbors as is true in more primitive societies. Our interdependence network is so large that we often feel lost and helpless. For example, for medical help, instead of a general practitioner, a family doctor we know and who knows us, we have access to the possibility of much better aid with specialists and large hospitals but at the cost of sometimes feeling confused and at the mercy of impersonal forces we do not understand.

Although we are so dependent on others, we still have the great myth of rugged individualism. We can buy our own insurance. We can drive our own car down to the unemployment office and collect our own unemployment compensation. We rely on insurance, savings, government, utility corporations, in other words, the system and not individuals. We can ignore the fact that behind the big structures it still really is individuals on whom we rely. But for many, there is no one close in time of need, and "the system" cannot supply all of our human needs.

According to Vance Packard, "Where technology is in a runaway stage, as in the United States, both mobility and general uprootedness tend to run highest."[2] Packard gives many statistics to document the uprootedness of our society. One that he quotes from the Journal of the American Statistical Association, (Sept. 1970) is that the average American moves about fourteen times in his lifetime; the average Briton about eight times; and the average Japanese about five times. Since this describes conditions in the 1960s, it may be even worse now. Why is the mobility higher in the United States than in the other two technologically advanced countries? It might be that the United States is more advanced technologically. However, I believe that it is more likely due to other values held by those countries. The British emphasis on tradition and the Japanese emphasis on family might slow the erosion of the community. Although the problem may be worse in the United States than elsewhere, it is a growing problem worldwide.

Communes or intentional communities are the answer for some

but not for all. Perhaps if the definition of intentional community were broad enough, that would be the answer for all. But then we would still have to construct that definition. Although the Biblical metaphor is that we are parts of a body, every person is unique. We are not all red blood cells nor all fatty tissue. So different models of community are needed for different parts of the body. In many cases the mobility of our society has destroyed the extended family, sometimes even the nuclear family, and also the community church fellowship. Therefore, we are in need of new models.

What is necessary for a community? What kinds and what levels of sharing are required? There can be no community without some continuity. How long term must the commitment be? How can one create community? What is the focus? For a Christian community, the obvious focus is Christ, but in what ways does that manifest itself?

Communities need to be small enough to be manageable and provide a sense of participation and individual significance. On the other hand, they must be large enough to provide security and support for those within the community and aid to those outside. What size is right for a given group? The boundaries must be flexible and changing, not a closed group. Jesus chose twelve for certain purposes but He always included others. And, even the twelve gave aid to the poor.

If a person has the mind of Christ, he has the humility and love required to give or accept aid as the circumstances require. So our attitude is an important factor in determining the length of time it takes to create community. Ideally, fellowship between Christians should be instantaneous. And to the extent that it depends on the Christian, that between a Christian and non-Christian should be instantaneous also. In the real world it never happens quite that fast.

A couple of years ago, a friend and I decided to share a second car. Our families were similar in size, five in one, six in the other. Because of employment of various members of each family, each sometimes required two cars, but not always. Therefore, we shared the ownership of one car while each owned another separately. We worked out the procedures for its use to our mutual satisfaction and it worked quite well. The strange thing about it was the comment of Christian friends that our arrangement was nice and worked because of our personalities, but it would not work for most. That seemed strange to me, not because I think everyone should share a car but because if the need arose, every Christian should be able to share something as unimportant as a car whatever his personality might be. In fact, if one's personality would cause problems, perhaps that person should have the experience of sharing. Our experiment with the shared car worked because I knew my friend was more concerned that I not be cheated and, I hope, because he knew I was more concerned that he not be cheated. The beauty of the sharing was, and always is, that each of us had something different to share with the other that produced benefits that would be impossible alone.

The "God is love" axiom implies that love is the basis for community. No force, physical, mental, or emotional, is used by the group to keep the group together. Love experienced within the community enables it to serve those outside. Just as the fellowship is characterized by compassion not coercion, so is its activity in working to solve problems in the world devoid of coercion but filled with compassion. The God of love told us that love never fails, even when it appears to fail from our human perspective. In fact, we must do what is right whether or not it seems "successful" and whether or not other people do it.

One of our actions that is inconsistent with our axioms is our incessant drive for money and material things at the expense of people and relationships. As a visitor from Indonesia observed about our society, "Everything travels so fast we can hardly find people who value cooperation, love, and understanding. They just value their time for money, money, money."[3] Similarly, a visitor from Bolivia said, "North Americans have to work more in order to buy things. For that reason they spend less time with their families, thinking that to be comfortable is more important for the family than to give them love and time together."[4]

An example of a decision of our society that tended to destroy community is the consolidation of schools. Small neighborhood high schools were destroyed so that more efficient (cost-effective) consolidations could be constructed. This allowed many good things to happen (for example, better equipped labs), but at a cost. The high school athletic teams won more championships, but fewer people could participate in inter-varsity competition. In the larger more impersonal setting there is less personal accountability and hence less responsibility. Teachers, students, and parents are not as well acquainted with each other. Misbehavior is easier, drug problems are worse.

Technology is one of these things that needs to be evaluated on the basis of what it does to community. For example, the Amish (a conservative branch of the Mennonite Church, whose roots go back to the Anabaptist movement of the Reformation), have strict regulations regarding the use of technology. They are often accused of being inconsistent when sometimes we just do not recognize their beginning assumptions. Of course, like all of us, they are sometimes inconsistent, too. But, given their axioms, we might find some apparently contradictory decisions are understandable, even though we might make different decisions because of slightly different axioms. Outsiders sometimes fail to see that one of their fundamental goals is the preservation of traditional family and community life. Riding in a rented car may be permitted while owning a car is not. If a car were evil in itself, this would be inconsistent. But if riding in a car permits one to visit relatives or friends, while owning a car would tend to weaken the family, perhaps this is consistent. If technology were inherently evil, then a gasoline engine used to cool milk and a gasoline engine on four rubber tires would both be wrong. But if one helps to keep a family farm concept strong while the other weakens it, then it is logical to accept one and reject the other. James J. Flick in *The Car Culture* states, "Ultimately, automobility made the small family farm obsolete."[5] However, Amish family farms are still doing a good job of supporting the family, even when most farmers are experiencing severe financial strain.

Although all Mennonites stress community, most do not emphasize it as much as the Amish. In November of 1984, however, a group of concerned Mennonite farmers met to discuss the current agricultural crisis. The following is from a committee report for that meeting. "We hear a call for a return to community. We have become separated from each other. We have lost the awareness of each other and mutual aid is weak. We confess that we have become increasingly individualistic and independent. We need to recognize the importance of cooperation and mutual support."[6]

Though they strongly promote community in many ways, I believe that the Amish violate one of my basic concepts of community. They require a standardized mode of attire and limited educational opportunities to help maintain social cohesion. These rules follow from the desire for community, but I believe (in connection with other of their traditions), brings in the element of coercion. Since the Amish must dress in a certain way or make a complete break with the community, they have little opportunity to make the kind of contacts they would need to know whether or not they wanted to leave the Amish community. So some traditions are coercive in nature. In building models for Christian community we must be careful not to include such traditions.

The Bruderhof movement, led by Eberhard Arnold, is a twentieth century attempt at communal living that is aware of this danger of coercion. Arnold said, "Our life is entirely voluntary...A voluntary life means that a person's will is set free for God and His Kingdom. This freedom of will leads to a free obedience born of faith and divine love."[7] He is also aware that a community must help others. "No community that exists for its own sake can survive...It would lose the way by becoming isolated, no matter how much it practiced community."[8] The Bruderhof leaders realized also the need for mutual submission and discipline. As a result they became affiliated with the Hutterites, an Anabaptist communal group which has been in existence since the sixteenth century. Unfortunately, their differences have caused them to separate.

In order to get an entirely different perspective on the problem of evaluating technology, imagine that a superhuman being from some distant galaxy visited the United States in the year 1900 with a proposal. It would give us the power to transport ourselves quickly, easily, and comfortably over long distances and a side effect would be a boost to our entire economic system. In return we need to supply an annual human sacrifice of 50,000 lives. Some small percent could be especially bad or irresponsible people, another small percent could be alcoholics, but mostly they would be chosen at random from the general population. Can you imagine the revulsion we would have felt and the speed with which we would have turned the proposal down! Yet, in effect, that is the result of our use of the automobile. In addition to over 50,000 fatalities per year, there are approximately 4,000,000 injured annually in the United States.[9]

I would like for you to consider whether or not our use of the automobile has been a wise course of action. Most people to whom I have suggested this idea have reacted at once that the car has been and is so useful that of course it is a good thing. But I believe we really need to think deeply about this, not that we are likely to change the use we make of the automobile, but because we need an example to see how important it is to evaluate technology before we develop and use it. We need something to counteract the mood that "if we can make it, we must" or "it's here, good or bad, so we must make the most of it." We need to see an example of a time when we should have made a different choice, so we will take more seriously evaluation and control of technology in the future. So, I am using the car as an example. Doubtless, there are many other possible examples.

Even today we take lightly the loss of life due to accidents. An editorial in our local paper stated that "last year the Indiana death toll dropped by more than 100 and since the last full year before [adoption of the 55 mph speed limit], 1973, the Indiana death toll on highways has declined by 453...We have to believe that the lowered speed limit has had something to do with the decline in the number of people killed on Indiana highways, streets and roads."[10] In spite of this, the editorial was supporting a change from 55 mph to 65 mph and gave no real reasons for doing so, except that there seemed to be no gasoline shortage then. There was a reference to complaints that some businesses might be damaged by the lower speed limits, but the editorialist didn't seem to believe that. In other words, we ought to be able to drive faster because we now have the gasoline to do so and in spite of the belief that more people will die as a result. Nearly 10,000 lives were saved annually in the United States due to the 55 mph speed limit.[11]

Many Christians disobey the law by driving faster than the speed limit and would support a law raising the limit. I can account for this only by supposing that they ignore or explain away the evidence that lives are saved by driving under 55 or simply refusing to think about it. In any case it seems to be a good example of actions inconsistent with axioms.

Another problem with cars is the rapid depletion of a nonrenewable resource. Even though presently we have enough gasoline, we are sure to run out at some date in the not so distant future. But as usual, we make choices on the basis of what is economical at the moment instead of distinguishing between renewable and nonrenewable resources or between polluting and non-polluting processes. Pollution, of course, is another one of the problems with automobiles.

Another effect of our use of cars is the deleterious effect it has had on family file. It has increased our individual mobility and so encouraged individual members of a family to go separate ways. It has contributed to parents having jobs that require more time spent away from home. The Lynd and Lynd study of Middletown reports,

"Instead of a family's activities in getting a living, making a home, play, church going and so on, largely overlapping and bolstering each other, one's neighbors may work at shops at the other end of the city, while those with whom one works may have their homes and other interests anywhere from one to two score miles distant."[12]

Flick concludes that the motor car was destructive of community and parental authority. "What the individual gained from automobile ownership was at the expense of undermining community and family, and it invited anonymity and anomie."[13] The capability of different family members to go their separate ways not only weakens family ties but also neighborhood ties since much more time is now spent outside the neighborhood in which one resides.

The car has contributed to the extramarital sexual activity of teen-agers, directly by providing more situations where it is more easily done and indirectly by the weakening of the family and community. A report by the Alan Guttmacher Institute reported that in 1980, 18% of the boys and 6% of the girls already engaged in sexual intercourse by the age of 14, most begin at 16 and it is a rare individual who has not by age 19. In contrast in the 1950s only 2% of the girls and 10% of the boys had intercourse by age 16.[14] According to psychologist Michael Campion, "Rape, divorce, open sexuality, venereal disease, and extra-marital affairs have increased markedly."[15]

According to a 1985 article in *Time* magazine, "If present trends continue, researchers estimate, fully 40% of today's 14-year old girls will be pregnant at least once before the age of 20."[16] And in the same article it was stated that "the incidence of sexual intercourse among teenage women increased by two-thirds during the 1970s."[17] Accord-ing to a 1988 study of young people who attend church regularly, 3% begin sexual activity by age 12, 17% by age 14, 26% by age 16, and 43% by age 18. These figures are only 10-15% below those for the general youth population.[18]

Of course there have been times of loose morality before, but it does seem probable that the automobile has contributed to this one, at least in its earlier stages. However, I believe that movies, TV, and popular songs probably have an even greater influence on morality than cars. According to the same *Time* article referred to earlier, "In a year the average viewer sees more than 9,000 scenes of suggested sexual intercourse or innuendo in prime time TV."[19] Remember that that was a 1985 article. The number would be even higher today and the scenes would be much more explicit.

Another of the bad effects of cars has been their contribution to an extreme individualism. This individualism, in turn, makes us value the individual family car, or cars even more. Thus it is even harder to evaluate its use fairly. That is, it makes us more individualistic, which interferes with our seeing its bad effects. Although more subtle than some of the car's other effects, this contribution to more individualism may be its most dangerous.

What about the good things automobiles do for us? In emergencies, they get us to the hospital fast and they do many other good things. I haven't discussed those because we are already familiar with them. The question is, is there more good than bad? Or a better question is, could we have used technology in other ways to have obtained its benefits and avoided its ill-effects? The answer to this is an overwhelming yes.

Sixty years ago, we had an inter-urban rail system that was electrically powered as well as an electrically powered street car system within the cities. This was less polluting than cars and in the long run much more economical. But in the short run, cars were cheaper and more convenient, allowing for much more individual freedom. Therefore we chose cars. We could have had various forms of rail transportation for long distances and light, electrically powered cars for short trips. This is one alternative that would not have contributed so much to the breakdown of family and neighborhood communities and to the excess of individualism. Flick similarly suggests, "From the perspective of hindsight, however, the best solution to urban transportation problems would have been a balanced commitment to motor trucks and motor buses along with rail transportation, rather than the mass ownership of private passenger cars in cities."[20] Another alternative to our current dependance on cars would be to limit their use in cities. In 1981, a new town of approximately 2,000 people was planned in Oregon in which cars were banned "in favor of bicycles, and a small trolley (train) system for public transport."[21]

It should be kept in mind that I am not raising these objections as an argument to abolish the internal combustion engine. It would be very expensive, disruptive of our whole economic structure, and virtually impossible. At some point we will be forced to do it, but we won't do it until then. The whole purpose is that I believe we need to see an example of a poor choice of technology so that we will work harder at evaluating instead of just doing whatever is possible and happens to be profitable at the time. The physicist Erwin Schrodinger said that the machine "must take over the toil for which man is too good, not man the work for which the machine is too expensive...This will not tend to make production cheaper but those who are engaged in it happier."[22]

As mentioned before, television has contributed to a decay in morality. If not handled with care, television may be disruptive of community in other ways, also,. How often do we use TV to keep the kids occupied, when we should be doing something with them, hiking, talking, playing games, developing constructive hobbies, or even working with them? Television allows little direct interaction between people, which may lead to loss of empathy or compassion. TV is not necessarily bad, but if not used properly could be hazardous to the health of a community.

More and more our culture is being created by television instead of local communities. TV personalities and TV show characters are more familiar to many than are neighbors, fellow church members, and relatives. "People no longer actually live in their own homes with their own families, in their local neighborhoods...They live in the house on the other side of the looking glass, the soap opera house. [Television stars] are their neighbors. They live in the anonymity of mobility and mediation."[23]

It might seem as if television would promote community because everyone has the same experience. But that could be one of its dangers. Remember that Christian community is not a collection of cloned individuals but a body of unique but harmonious parts. When we all see the same program, we may not need to communicate about it. (It depends on the type of program; some are very stimulating and could lead to much discussion.) In any case, for community to be valuable each individual must bring unique experiences to the group and a willingness and ability to communicate with others.

Every labor saving device must be examined to determine its effect on community. For example, a man buys a riding lawn mower to save time and effort. Suppose that this man has a job that requires a minimum of physical effort. Our man realizes that he needs some exercise so he buys weights to lift, a jogging outfit, or joins an exercise club. All of this takes money, hence time to make that money and makes him spend time away from his family. In this case, he may have been better off spending more time in his yard working with his children and having time to visit with his neighbor. As another example, should a man buy his wife an automatic dishwasher or spend more time helping her wash dishes? Which one promotes community the most?

Francis Schaeffer has described how the women in the villages of Switzerland, when he first moved there, washed clothes at village pumps in cold water. His first reaction was that it was an awful shame, but then he said, "Gradually a different idea dawned on me—working at the fountain took up a lot of the woman's day, but she spent the time talking with other village women, doing a necessary job; she existed in a very human setting. Was that worse than a woman in the United States . . . who has a great number of labor saving devices. . . but spends all her time being morose and lonely? The question is, what does she do with the time she saves? If she spends all her time just doing nothing or destroying herself and her family, wouldn't she be better off washing at the village pump in the cold water?"[24]

He also tells about the women out in the fields working with their husbands. Again, his first reaction was pity for them because they did not have as easy a life as American women. But then he changed his mind completely, saying: "The women who worked with their husbands shoulder to shoulder during the day and then slept with them at night had one of the greatest riches in the world. Is anything worse than our modern affluent situation where the wife has no share in the real life of her husband?"[25]   Remember the point is not that all technology and all labor saving devices are bad, but that in every case their use should be carefully evaluated in the light of what it does for or against community.

One purpose of this chapter has been to identify a few basic Christian axioms and to explore some of their implications concerning community. I realize that I have raised more questions than I have answered, but I believe I have indicated a few general characteristics of Christian community. Perhaps the main purpose is to get people to think about whether or not their lifestyles are consistent with their basic beliefs.

I would like to close this chapter by considering the values of community. If God is love and we are created in His image, then our happiness and well being depend on giving and receiving love. So one very important value is that only in community can we experience the highest good for which God has created us. Not only does this follow from our axioms but our experience bears it out also. Think of your happiest moments and most contented times. Don't they all involve relationships with people? Even the good things that have happened to us not involving other people were enhanced by sharing them with loved ones or spoiled because we had no one to share them with.

> C.S. Lewis tells us about one more value of Christian community: God can show Himself as He really is only to real men. And that means not simply to men who are individually good, but to men who are united together in a body, loving one another, helping one another, showing Him to one another. For that is what God meant humanity to be like; like players in one band, or organs in one body. Consequently, the one really adequate instrument for learning about God is the whole Christian community, waiting for Him together. Christian brotherhood is, so to speak, the technical equipment for this science—the laboratory outfit.[26]

Therefore, for these reasons, community is not an option for a Christian. It is a requirement.

Postulates, Paradoxes, and Pacifism

"The gospel and its adherents are not to be protected by the sword,
nor are they thus to protect themselves...Neither do they use worldly
sword or war, since all killing has ceased with them."

Conrad Grebel

How can it be that Christians disagree on such an important issue as that of participation or non-participation in warfare? Of course, it is true that Christians disagree on many questions. Conflicting conclusions result from either different postulates (i.e. axioms or assumptions) or faulty reasoning. Discussion within the Christian community ought to help us discover false postulates and incorrect logic.

The necessity of loving others is the most basic postulate for every aspect of the Christian life. The Old Testament set a high standard. "You shall love your neighbor as yourself" (Lev. 19:18). And yet, the New Testament goes beyond that in two ways. Jesus said, "A new command I give you: Love one another. As I have loved you, so you must love one another" (John 13:34, NIV). As we have seen, to love as Christ loved us is a higher level of love than to love as we love ourselves. The second way is that a broader love is demanded of us because Jesus also said, "Love your enemies, do good to those who hate you" (Luke 6:27). I think that this is an example of parallel thoughts that occur so often in Hebrew poetry. To love is to do good. An enemy is one who hates us.

So we must start with the postulate that we are to be committed to work and sacrifice to promote the welfare of others, even our enemies. Now punishment is not incompatible with love, so this love postulate does not unequivocally imply pacifism. Still, death is a pretty extreme form of punishment. I find it difficult to reconcile killing a fellow Christian with loving him and his family and friends. Furthermore, I have even more difficulty combining a belief in hell with the killing of a non-Christian.

Parenthetically, I am using pacifism as a general term meaning a belief that killing another person even in a declared war is wrong, and just war theory as the position that Christians may participate in some wars if certain conditions are met. There are many varieties of pacifism and many variations of the just war theory. For purposes of this discussion we do not need to go into these finer differentiations.

Another Christian postulate is that our actions must be based on Biblical principles. In the Sermon on the Mount, Jesus said,

> You have heard that it was said, 'An eye for an eye and a tooth for a tooth.' But I say to you, Do not resist one who is evil. But if anyone strikes you on the right cheek, turn to him the other also;...You have heard that it was said, 'You shall love your enemies and pray for those who persecute you, so that you may be sons of your father who is in heaven; for he makes his sun rise on the evil and on the good, and sends rain on the just and on the unjust...You, therefore, must be perfect, as your heavenly Father is perfect" (Matt. 5:38, 39, 43, 44, 48).

One interpretation is that this passage is about private actions only and has nothing to do with war. That is, as individuals we are to turn the other cheek, but as part of a nation we need not do so. However, according to the commentator William Barclay, the eye for an eye principle "was never a law which gave a private individual the right to extract vengeance; it was always a law which laid down how a judge in the law court must assess punishment and penalty (cp. Deuteronomy 19:18). This law was never intended to give the individual person the right to indulge even in the vengeance of tit for tat."[1] So it must be dealing with more than just individual ethics.

Another passage that, I believe, points toward the pacifist position is found in Romans 12. "Do not repay evil for evil. Be careful to do what is right in the eyes of everybody. If it is possible, as far as it depends on you, live at peace with everyone. Do not take revenge, my friends, but leave room for God's wrath, for it is written: 'It is mine to avenge; I will repay,' says the Lord. On the contrary: 'If your enemy is hungry, feed him; if he is thirsty, give him something to drink. In doing this, you will heap burning coals on his head.' Do not be overcome by evil, but overcome evil with good" (Rom. 12:17-21, NIV).

In reply to some of Pilate's questions, Jesus answered, "My king-ship is not of this world; if my kingship were of this world, my servants would fight, that I might not be handed over to the Jews; but my king-ship is not from the world" (John 18:36). Paul said, "For though we live in the world we do not wage war as the world does. The weapons we fight with are not the weapons of the world. On the contrary, they have divine power to demolish strongholds" (II Cor. 10:3-4).

Many other passages support the pacifist view as well. On the other hand, there are many passages that could be cited against the pacifist position. I believe that the whole spirit of the New Testament teaching on love can only lead to pacifism. However, in this chapter I cannot take the time and space to further support that claim. I can only ask the readers to study the entire New Testament to evaluate that claim for themselves. I will have more to say about these paradoxes within the New Testament later. I believe that they are minor compared to the apparent contradiction on this issue between the Old and New Testa-ments. I believe that if we had the New Testament only, it would be clear that pacifism is the correct view. But if we had the Old Testament only, pacifism would not even be considered. How can we resolve this paradox?

The Old Testament is filled with stories of bloodshed and warfare carried on by men of God. In many cases it is said that God is com-manding them to do so. In the first place, the Old Testament poses problems for many people besides pacifists. For example, the take-over of Palestine by the Jews does not fit into the just war category. Thus, just war advocates have a problem. And if the Old Testament is used against pacifism, then it could be used to defend the killing of babies as the following passage shows. Samuel told Saul, "This is what the Lord Almighty says: 'I will punish the Amalekites for what they did to Israel when they waylaid them as they came up from Egypt. Now go, attack the Amalekites and totally destroy everything that be-longs to them. Do not spare them; put to death men and women, chil-dren and infants, cattle and sheep, camels and donkeys'" (I Sam. 15:2-

3).

The Old Testament says that God commands the death penalty for a variety of transgressions: enticing others to idolatry (Deut. 13:6-11), working on the Sabbath (Numbers 15:32-26), fornication (Deut. 22:20-21), being a disobedient son (Deut. 21:18-21), and keeping a mean ox (Ex. 21:29)! Most Christians would not argue that we should have the death penalty for those actions today. Many Christians would not even consider some of those things sins today.

Perhaps the Old Testament characters misunderstood what God was telling them. Perhaps there are different dispensations. It would seem as though God might expect more of us since through Jesus Christ we have a fuller revelation of the nature of God than they had. About many things Jesus said, "It was said...but I say." In each case, I believe, Jesus was moving us beyond the statement of the law in the direction of the spirit of the law.

The author of Hebrews clearly states that the old covenant is obsolete and is replaced by a new one.

> The ministry Jesus has received is as superior to theirs as the covenant of which he is mediator is superior to the old one...For if there had been nothing wrong with that covenant, no place would have been sought for another. But God found fault with the people and said: 'The time is coming...when I will make a new covenant...It will not be like the old covenant...This is the covenant I will make with the house of Israel,...I will put my laws in their minds and write them on their hearts. I will be their God and they will be my people...' By calling this covenant 'new,' he has made the first one obsolete; and what is obsolete and aging will soon disappear (Heb. 8:6-13).

I certainly don't know the complete answer to this paradox, but I cannot put what the prophets said on the same level as what Jesus said. I will use the Prince of Peace to interpret the prophets and not the other way around. That is, my postulate is that in any apparent conflict between Old and New Testament, I will give more weight to the New.

Before leaving this subject of the Old Testament, I should point out that even in it there are hints that man's involvement in war is not

His highest will. God did not allow David to build the temple because he was a man of war. Most battles were won by God's intervention, not by man's might. It might even be that if the Israelites had been faithful, they would not have had to fight at all (See Ex. 23:20-30).

There are some indications in the New Testament that it is permissible to participate in wars. For example, soldiers are not told to resign from the army. However, slave owners are not told to free their slaves either, but we would not argue that Christians should own slaves. Another example is found in chapter 13 of Romans where we are told to submit to the governing authorities. However, this comes right after the strong statements in chapter 12 about not repaying evil with evil and feeding your enemies instead of taking revenge. I think Jesus clarified this relationship when He pointed out that Caesar had a right to money since his image was on it, but God has a right to us because His image is on us. It is also clear that in any disagreement between God's law and man's law, we must obey God.

Another problem with pacifism is that most Christians for nearly 2,000 years have not been pacifists. Church tradition is powerful, but by itself does not prove anything. After all, the reformers rebelled against beliefs held by the church for over a thousand years. This long just war tradition in the church is, in my mind, more than offset by the position of the early church, which was pacifist.

The book *War and Christian Ethics*, edited by Arthur Holmes gives the positions on this issue of church leaders in their own words. The early leaders are all against killing. Origen, who lived from 185-254 said, "None fight better for the king than we do. We do not indeed fight under him, although he require it; but we fight on his behalf, forming a special army—an army of piety—by offering our prayers to God."[2] In the third century, the Canons of Hippolytus enacted that "a soldier of civil authority must be taught not to kill men and to refuse to do so if he is commanded."[3]

This latter quotation shows that the early church leaders opposed Christians being soldiers because of killing, not just because the Roman army required worship of the emperor, as some have claimed. According to the church historian Roland Bainton,

> The pacifism of the early church was derived not from a New Testament legalism, but from an effort to apply what was the mind of Christ…the thought of these fathers was closer to the New Testament than to that of succeeding periods, namely, that they operated almost exclusively with New Testament concepts without drawing so heavily as did later generations on classical and Old Testament themes…The primary ground of their aversion was the conviction of its incompatibility with love. The quality of love set forth by Jesus and by Paul had not been lost in the early church.[4]

After Constantine, the situation changed drastically, with the state seemingly taking over the church. Eventually, instead of no Christians in the army, no non-Christians could be in the army. The evolution of the attitude toward war went from pacifism to "we can't fight to protect Christianity or self, only to protect other people's lives" to "we can fight to protect property and Christianity." The evolution of the "just war" theory is interesting but beyond the scope of this treatment.

From 300 to 1500 only isolated individuals or small groups were pacifists. In the early sixteenth century, the Anabaptists, later called Mennonites, held the pacifist position as a church. So did the Church of the Brethren from the seventeenth century and the Quakers or Friends from the eighteenth century. Through the years, individuals in other Protestant churches and in the Catholic Church have also been pacifist. According to John Howard Yoder, "The pacifist thrust was well represented by Dwight L. Moody and by Jonathan Blanchard, founder of Wheaton College, as well as by earlier revivalists."[5] After the controversy between "fundamentalists" and "social gospel" adherents, "the pacifism of Blanchard and Moody was removed from the record by their heirs."[6]

Where church tradition is assumed (postulated) to be determinative, the just war theory is held. Again according to Yoder, "The phenomenon of pacifism tends to arise wherever there is church renewal. Pacifism arises where people are trying to be Christian without too much rootage in history."[7] As an example, he gives "the restoration movement" of the early nineteenth century from which came denominations called "Disciples" or "Christians." Alexander Campbell was an early leader, and he took the pacifist position as a number of people in these churches still do. Another example he gives is the Churches of God.

Does reason support pacifism? Many say that it is not practical, but that is said about most, if not all, of the Sermon on the Mount. If Jesus taught pacifism, then the question of practicality is irrelevant. We must obey God. However, I would like to consider briefly the reasonableness or unreasonableness of pacifism without the assumption of any command from God.

There are situations where it seems obvious that if someone isn't killed or war isn't declared, a terrible injustice will occur, an innocent person or perhaps many innocent people will be killed. However, we never know for sure what will happen in the future. And we have evidence that when people resort to violence, they often become like the people they are fighting. Many times idealistic groups have rebelled against tyrannical governments and by using deceit and violence have overthrown the original government, only to find that they had become as evil as their former oppressors.

Martin Luther King, Jr. and Gandhi were killed; does that mean nonviolence does not work? Bonhoeffer was involved in an attempt to assassinate Hitler and was killed; does that mean violence does not work? Many say that King and Gandhi were at least partially successful, but only because their opponents, Americans and Englishmen were Christians and that their methods would not work, for example, in Nazi Germany. First of all, some of the things done to people in India and to Afro-Americans could hardly be said to be done by Christians and second, there were Germans who were Christians. Gandhi insisted that non-violent resistance should have been used against Hitler. If it had been, many Jews and others would have been killed, but it is hard to imagine that more would have been killed than were without non-violent resistance!

In fact, we have an example of non-violent resistance against the Nazis. The Danes refused to cooperate with and protested against persecution of the Jews. When the Germans tried to introduce the yellow badge to identify Jews, the King of Denmark said he would be the first to wear it. Danish government officials said that if there were any anti-Jewish measures, they would resign. When the Germans tried to round up the Jews, they were hidden by their Danish neighbors, and then the Danes themselves financed the escape of the Jews to Sweden by ship. This non-violent resistance had an effect on the hardened Nazi officials.

> Politically and psychologically, the most interesting aspect of this incident is perhaps the role played by the German authorities in Denmark, their obvious sabotage of orders from Berlin. It is the only case we know of in which the Nazis met with open native resistance, and the result seems to have been that those exposed to it changed their minds...They had met resistance based on principle, and their 'toughness' had melted like butter in the sun, they had even been able to show a few timid beginnings of genuine courage.[8]

This is not to say that non-violence will always "work" from a human point of view, but neither does violence always "work." We do know that in the long run "love never fails." In II Cor. 10:3-4, cited earlier, Paul said that we do not use the world's weapons, but the weapons we use have "divine power to demolish strongholds." What if the amount of effort going into war planning went into planning for peace? In 1985, the world was spending $1.3 billion per day on armaments while fifty thousand people starved to death each day.[9] In the fiscal year 1989 the U.S. alone budgeted over $0.8 billion per day for defense.[10] If we spent only a small fraction of this money on non-violent methods of achieving peace and justice, who can say what the results would be? If there were less injustice in the world, there would be less probability of war. Communism spread more by infiltration made possible by injustice than by military action.

If you turn the other cheek, the aggressor might repent; on the other hand, he might kill you. The important thing is, what does Christ expect of us? There are paradoxes in the Bible on this question, but as we have seen there are paradoxes in science and even in mathematics. In this life, it seems that we must live with paradox, but we do have reason and the Holy Spirit to help us resolve them. From my postulates among which are that God is love, that the Bible is a reliable guide, that the New Testament gives us a clearer revelation of God than the Old Testament, and that the early church had good insight into the mind of Christ, I believe that pacifism is the valid conclusion. I believe that the Holy Spirit has helped me to this conclusion, but am also aware that I could be mistaken. My prayer is that I will always be open to correction. I also pray that all Christians will consider their postulates and evaluate the just war hypothesis and the pacifism hypothesis, in the light of Biblical data with the help of the Holy Spirit and God given reason.

Knowledge, Love, Obedience

"Day by day, three things I pray,
To see Thee more clearly,
To love Thee more dearly,
To follow Thee more nearly."
From the musical *Godspell*

In this short concluding chapter, I would like to summarize what I believe are some of the most important points in this book. These points are about how a person may evaluate the claim that Christianity is true, how a Christian should live, and how a Christian can help unbelievers.

God gave us the ability to reason so that we could understand things more clearly. It can be an aid on the path to faith. God does not ask us to believe the impossible. Christianity is a reasonable religion. Our reason, imagination, and experience used with humility help us to see as God sees. The most effective thing that Christians can do to help unbelievers to belief is to show forth God's love within the Christian community and through that community to all those who come into contact with it. Transformed Christians' lives are the best witness for the truth of Christianity.

As we see God more clearly, we not only love Him more dearly, but we get our minds off of ourselves so that we are able to love others. Reason can help us to understand what love is and thus make our love more effective.

The more we love God, the more we want to know Him better and the more motivation we have to follow Him more nearly. It is in the fellowship of believers that we can best experience His love, and as C.S. Lewis pointed out, the Christian community is the best instrument to teach us about God and His will for our lives. The support of other believers is a powerful aid to obedience.

Understanding the importance of assumptions (axioms or postulates) can be a help in withstanding the pressures of our society. The

Kingdom of God's axioms are that God is love, we are to love Him with everything we have, and we are to love others as Christ has loved us. Understanding those axioms and what love really is, we can see how different the Kingdom of God is from the kingdom of this world. We can only understand love by seeing examples and we have the supreme example in the incarnation, life, and death of Jesus Christ. Not only can we then see the difference between the Kingdom of God and the world, but the grace of God can transform our lives so that others can see also.

What advice can we give to a person who does not know, but would like to know, if Christianity is true? The advice that is found in several of George MacDonald's novels is the best that I know. And that is, to start by reading the Gospels to see what Jesus said. If what He said makes any sense, then obey that much. I believe that much Jesus said will ring true to anyone with an open mind. As we obey that little bit, we will be opening ourselves to receive more truth. Those truths will involve service to others, and the upward spiral will have begun. As we see Him more clearly, we will love Him more dearly, and follow Him more nearly, and as we follow Him more nearly, we will see Him more clearly, and so on ad infinitum. Wherever we are on the spiral we can will to do His will, which will enable His grace to empower us to love and obey at ever higher levels.

A fitting close to this short summary chapter is a few verses from the hymn, "Speak Now, O God, To Hearts Unmoved and Cold" by M. Elmore Turner.

> O Grant us wisdom Lord, Thy will to see;
> Show us the path of true humility;
> May we do justly, led by mercy's hand,
> Obedient to Thy Spirit's high command.
>
> Guide Thou our feet to ministries of love;
> Grant us compassion like to Thine above;
> Cause us to set the blind and captive free
> To find in Christ the Lord their liberty.

Nerve us, O Lord, to face the times of strain;
Our hands in loyal works of love sustain;
Help us to live, with Christlike vision clear,
In partnership, to bring Thy Kingdom near.

Part I - Faith and Reason

Chapter 1 - Introduction

1. John Updike. *Pigeon Feathers and Other Stories.* (Greenwich, Conn.: Fawcett Publications, Inc., 1962), p. 84-105.
2. Karl R. Popper. *Conjectures and Refutations: the Growth of Scientific Knowledge.* (NY: Harper & Row, Publishers, 1963), p. 152-3.

Chapter 2 - Truth and Reality

1. David Elton Trueblood, *General Philosophy.* (NY: Harper & Row, Publishers, 1963), pp. 46-68.
2. Morris Kline. *Mathematics and the Search for Knowledge.* (New York: Oxford University Press, 1985), p. 19.
3. James Como. ed. *At the Breakfast Table.* (NY: Macmillan, 1988), p. 146.
4. This quotation is by Russell Kirk from page 25 in *The Intercollegiate Review.* Fall/Winter, 1980.
5. Stephen Vincent Benet. *John Brown's Body.* (Garden City, NY: Nelson Doubleday, Inc., 1969), p. vii.
6. Paul M. VanBuren. *The Edges of Language.* (NY: The Macmillan Company, 1972), p. 13-14.
7. Ibid. p. 30.
8. John Senior. *The Death of Christian Culture.* (New Rochelle, NY: Arlington House Publishers, 1978), p. 98. The quotation within the quotation is by John Ruskin.

Chapter 3 - Knowledge and Certainty

1. Arthur Holmes. *All Truth is God's Truth.* (Grand Rapids, MI: William B. Eerdmans Publishing Co., 1977), p. 106.
2. Karl R. Popper. *Conjectures and Refutations: The Growth of Scientific Knowledge.* (NY: Harper and Row, Publishers, 1965), p. 108.
3. C.S. Lewis. *Of This and Other Worlds.* (London: William

Collins Sons & Company, Ltd., 1982), p. 19.

4. Ibid. p. 73.

5. Leon Morris. *Testaments of Love*. (Grand Rapids, MI: William B. Eerdmans Publishing Company, 1981), p. 117.

6. Popper. p. 238.

Chapter 4 - Mathematical Certainty

1. Albert Einstein. *Essays in Science*. (NY: Philosophical Library, 1934), p. 13

2. Crane Brinton, Ed., *The Portable Age of Reason Reader*. (NY: The Viking Press, 1963), p. 129.

3. Thomas H. Greer. *A Brief History of Western Man*. (NY: Harcourt, Brace and World, Inc., 1968), p. 395.

4. Brinton. p. 129.

5. Ibid. p. 259

6. Abraham Lincoln. *The Collected Works of Abraham Lincoln*. (New Brunswick, New Jersey: Rutgers University Press, 1953), Vol. III, p. 375.

7. One such textbook is the following:
   Edwin Moise. *Elementary Geometry From An Advanced Standpoint*, 2nd Edition. (Reading, Massachusetts: Addison Wesley, 1974), Chapter 9.

8. Morris Kline. *Mathematics: The Loss of Certainty*. (NY: Oxford University Press, 1980), p. 312.

9. Ibid. p. 312.

10. Sir Thomas Heath. *The Thirteen Books of Euclid's Elements with Introduction and Commentary*, 2nd Edition. (NY: Dover, 1965, Vol. I), p. 153.

11. Howard Eves and Carroll Newsom. *An Introduction to the Foundation and Fundamental Concepts of Mathematics*. (NY: Holt, Rinehart and Winston, 1968), p. 305.

Chapter 5 - Scientific Fact

1. Leo Tolstoy. *What Then Must We Do*. (NY: Oxford University

Press, 1950), p. 237-8.

2. Herbert Butterfield. *The Origins of Modern Science*, Rev. Ed. (NY: The Free Press, 1965), p. 19.

3. Morris Kline. *Mathematics and the Search for Knowledge.* (NY: Oxford University Press, 1985), p. 81.

4. Reuben Hersh. *What is Mathematics, Really?.* (NY: Oxford University Press, 1997),   p. 209-10.

5. Robert Jastrow. *God and the Astronomers.* (NY: Warner Books, Inc., 1978), p. 17.

6. Ibid. p. 102.

7. Ibid. p. 103.

8. Ibid. p. 5.

9. Alfred North Whitehead. *Science and the Modern World.* (NY: The New American Library, 1948), p. 19.

10. Werner Heisenberg. *Physics and Beyond.* (NY: Harper and Row, 1972), p. 186.

11. Ronald W. Clark. *Einstein: The Life and Times.* (World Publishing Co., 1971), p. 94.

12. Denis Alexander. *Beyond Science.* (NY: A. J. Holman Company, 1972), p. 100.

13. Hilaire Cuny. *Albert Einstein, The Man and His Theories.* (Greenwich, Conn.: Fawcett Publications, Inc., 1962), p. 149.

14. Ibid. pp. 55-6.

15. This is one of the essays in *Essays in Science* by Einstein referred to earlier.

16. Bertrand Russell. *Mysticism and Logic.* (London: George Allen & Unwin LTD, 1959), p. 11.

17. Ibid. p. 9

18. Ibid. p. 12.

19. Ibid. p. 13

Chapter 6 - Gospel Truth

1. Ed. L. Miller, Ed. *Classical Statements of Faith and Reason.* (NY: Random House, 1970), p. 105, 113.

2. Blaise Pascal. *Pensees*. Any edition should have his "thoughts" numbered. This quotation comes from thought number 571.

3. F. F. Bruce. *The New Testament Documents: Are They Reliable?* (Downers Grove, IL: InterVarsity Press, 1972), p. 65.

4. C. S. Lewis. *Miracles*. (NY: The Macmillan Co., 1974), p. 113.

5. C. S. Lewis. *Mere Christianity*. (New York: The Macmillan Co., 1960), p. 41.

6. James Smith to Herndon, Jan. 24, 1867, first published in *Springfield Daily Illinois Journal*, March 12, 1867. James Smith was pastor of the church in Springfield, IL where Mary Lincoln was a member.

7. Werner Heisenberg. *Physics and Beyond*. p. 216

8. Again C. S. Lewis is helpful in the understanding of some of these problems, in particular *The Problem of Pain* and also his novel *Till We Have Faces*. The latter sheds light on the paradox of justice and mercy.

9. Elton Trueblood. *A Place to Stand*. (NY: Harper and Row, 1969), p. 20.

10. Denis Alexander. *Beyond Science*. p. 109.

11. Will Durant. *The Story of Philosophy*. (NY: Simon and Schuster, 1953), p. 337-8.

12. C. S. Lewis. *Mere Christianity*. p. 127.

13. Ibid. p. 128

14. Toyohiko Kagawa. *Love, The Law of Life*. (Chicago, IL: The John C. Winston Co., 1929), p. 310.

15. Bertrand Russell. *Mysticism and Logic*. (London: Allen and Unwin Ltd., 1959), p. 9, 12.

16. John Paul Von Grueningen, Ed. *Toward a Christian Philosophy of Higher Education*. (Westminster Press, 1957), p. 59.

17. Blaise Pascal. p. 282.

18. Von Grueningen. p. 60.

19. Denis Alexander. p. 182.

Chapter 7 - Beauty and Truth

1. Thomas S. Kuhn. _The Copernican Revolution._ (Cambridge, MA: Harvard University Press, 1975), p. 172.
2. Morris Kline. _Mathematics and the Search for Knowledge._ (NY: Oxford University Press, 1985), p. 70.
3. Ibid. p. 82.
4. Ronald W. Clark. _Einstein: The Life and Times._ (NY: World Publishing Co., 1971), p. 278.
5. John Polkinghorne. _One World._ (Princeton, NJ: Princeton University Press, 1986), p. 46.
6. Judith Wechsler, Ed. _On Aesthetics in Science._ (Cambridge, MA: Berkhauser Boston, 1988).
7. Martin Goldstein and Inge F. Goldstein. _How We Know._ (NY: Plenum Press, 1978), p. 4.
8. Paul Hoffman. "The Man Who Loves Numbers" _The Atlantic._ (Nov. 1987), p. 68.
9. Kline. p. 78.
10. Ibid. p. 123.
11. Ibid. p. 124.
12. Hugh Ross. _The Fingerprint of God_, 2nd. ed. (Orange, CA: Promise Publishing Co., 1991),   p. 112.
13. C.T. Andrews. _Mahatma Gandhi's Ideas._ (NY: The Macmillan Co., 1930), p. 334.
14. D. Elton Trueblood. _Philosophy of Religion._ (NY: Harper & Row, Publishers, 1957), p. 130.

Chapter 8 - Imagination and Reality

1. Morris Kline. _Mathematics and the Search for Knowledge._ (NY: Oxford University Press, 1985), p. 220.
2. Karl R. Popper. _Conjectures and Refutations: The Growth of Scientific Knowledge._ (NY: Harper & Row, Publishers, 1968), p. 95.
3. Ibid. p. 65.
4. Michael Guillen. _Bridges to Infinity: The Human Side of_

Mathematics. (Los Angeles: Jeremy P. Tarcher, Inc., distributed by Houghton Mifflin, 1983), p. 71.

5. Morris Kline. *Mathematics: The Loss of Certainty.* (New York: Oxford University Press, 1980), p. 312.

6. C. S. Lewis. *Of This and Other Worlds.* (London: William Collins Sons & Co. Ltd., 1980), p. 39.

Chapter 9 - A Fourth Dimension

1. The first extrapolation assumes that the nth term is given by 2n, the second assumes the nth term is 2^n, while the third assumes that it is given by $5n - n^2 - 2$.

2. For anyone interested in learning a little bit more about this, there is a good pamphlet (only 28 pages) written by Adrien L. Hess and published by the National Council of Teachers of Mathematics, entitled *Four-Dimensional Geometry, An Introduction.*

3. William G. Pollard. *Science and Faith: Twin Mysteries.* (NY: Thomas Nelson Inc., 1970), p. 84.

4. Ibid. p. 85.

5. Edwin A. Abbott. *Flatland.* (NY: Dover Publications, Inc., 1952). There are also some short stories that help supply some insight into the fourth dimension, "The Captured Cross Section" by Bruer in *Fantasia Mathematica* edited by Clifton Fadiman, Simon & Schuster and "Mimsy Were the Borogoves" by Padget in *Science Hall of Fame*, Vol. 1, edited by Robert Silverberg, Doubleday.

6. Henry P. Manning, Ed. *The Fourth Dimension Simply Explained.* (NY: Dover Publications, Inc., 1960).

7. Rudy Rucker. *The Fourth Dimension.* (Boston: Houghton Mifflin Co., 1984).

8. Manning. p. 40.

9. William G. Pollard. p. 26.

Chapter 10 - Higher Dimensions and Christianity

1. C. S. Lewis. *The Weight of Glory.* (Grand Rapids, Michigan: William B. Eerdmans Publishing Company, 1949), p. 23.

2. C. S. Lewis. *The Dark Tower and Other Stories.* (NY: Harcourt, Brace Jovanovich, 1977).

Chapter 11 - Faith and Obedience

1. Paul Tillich. *The New Being.* (New York: Charles Scribner's, 1955), p. 38.

2. E. Stanley Jones. *Is the Kingdom of God Realism?* (New York: Abingdon-Cokesbury Press, 1981), p. 193.

3. George MacDonald. *Weighed and Wanting.* (Boston: D. Lothrop Company, 1893), p. 373.

4. George MacDonald.

5. Jones. p. 194.

6. George MacDonald. *The Vicar's Daughter.* (London: Sampson Low, Marston Searle, & Rivington, 1881), pp. 271-3.

Part II - Love and Logic

Chapter 1 - Introduction

1. J. B. Phillips. *Making Men Whole.* (London: Fontana Books, 1959), p. 43.

2. Leon Morris. *Testaments of Love.* (Grand Rapids, MI: Eerdmans, 1981), p. 136.

3. Ibid. p. 136.

4. Ibid. pp. 142-43.

5. Ibid. p. 144.

6. Ibid. p. 167.

Chapter 2 - Logic

1. William Barclay. *The Gospel of John.* Rev. Ed. (Philadelphia, PA: The Westminster Press, 1975), pp. 35-36.

2. Leon Morris. *The Gospel According to John.* (Grand Rapids, MI: William B. Eerdmans Publishing Co., 1971), p. 123.

Chapter 3 - The Meaning of Love

1. Henry Drummond. *The Greatest Thing in the World and Other Addresses.* (NY: Fleming H. Revell Co., 1898), p. 23.
2. Paul Tillich. *Love, Power and Justice.* (NY: Oxford University Press, 1974), p. 26.
3. C. S. Lewis. *Mere Christianity.* (NY: Macmillan, 1958), p. 100.
4. Ibid. p. 101.
5. George MacDonald. *Guild Court.* (Philadelphia: David McKay, Publisher), p. 174.
6. E. Stanley Jones. *Christian Maturity.* (NY: Abingdon Press, 1957), p. 67.
7. Madeleine L'Engle. *A Circle of Quiet.* (Greenwich, CT: Fawcett Publications, Inc., 1972), p. 186.
8. Thomas Merton. *No Man Is An Island.* (Garden City, NY: Doubleday & Co., Inc., 1967), p. 133.
9. Richard J. Foster. *Freedom of Simplicity.* (San Francisco, CA: Harper & Row, Publishers, 1981), p. 42.
10. Charles Colson. *Loving God.* (Grand Rapids, MI: Zondervan, 1983), p. 126.

Chapter 4 - Analyses of Love

1. This analysis can be found in chapter one of *Four Loves* by C. S. Lewis. More of my ideas than I am even aware of come from Lewis.
2. C. S. Lewis. *Four Loves.* (NY: Harcourt, Brace and World, Inc., 1960), p. 33.
3. C. S. Lewis. *Poems.* (London: Geoffrey Bles, 1964), p. 134.
4. George MacDonald. *Donal Grant.* (Boston: Lothrop Publishing Co., 1883), p. 226.
5. George MacDonald. *What's Mine's Mine.* (London: Kegan,

Paul, Trench, Trubner & Co., Ltd., 1900), pp. 13-14.

6. Leo Tolstoy. *Last Diaries*. (New York: G.P. Putnam's Sons, 1960), p. 202.

7. For more on these Greek words for love, see the *Interpreter's Dictionary of the Bible, McKenzie's Dictionary of the Bible,* or *Kittel's Theological Dictionary*.

8. C. S. Lewis. *Mere Christianity*. (NY: The Macmillan Co., 1960), p. 85.

9. Leo Tolstoy. *Childhood, Boyhood and Youth*. (London: Oxford University Press, 1957), p. 307-8.

10. Ibid. p. 308.

Chapter 5 - The Best Love, Logic

1. C. S. Lewis. *The Four Loves*. NY: Harcourt, Brace and World, Inc., 1960)

2. Elton Trueblood. *The Company of the Committed*. (NY: Harper and Row, 1961), p. 98.

3. George MacDonald. *The Marquis of Lossie*. (London: Kegan, Paul, Trench, Trubner & Co., Ltd.), p. 159-60.

4. Richard J. Oglesby to William H. Herndon on January 5, 1866, quoted on p. 171 in *Lincoln Herald*, Winter 1977.

5. MacDonald. p. 124.

Chapter 6 - The Best Logic, Love

1. Madeleine L'Engle. *A Circle of Quiet*. (San Francisco: Harper & Row, 1972) p. 242-3..

Chapter 7 - Humility

1. CS. Lewis. *Mere Christianity*. (NY: The Macmillan Company, 1958), p. 94.

2. C. S. Lewis. *The Great Divorce*. (NY: The Macmillan Company, 1968), p. 62.

3. Ibid. p. 76.

4. Lewis. *Mere Christianity*. p. 96-7.

5. Francis A. Schaeffer. *No Little People*. (Downers Grove, IL: InterVarsity Press, 1979), p. 183.

6. Lewis. *Mere Christianity*. p. 98-9.

7. Leo Tolstoy. *Resurrection*. (NY: Penguin Books, 1985), p. 399.

8. Thomas Merton. *Seeds of Contemplation*. (NY: Dell Publishing Company, Inc., 1949), p. 39.

9. Ibid. p. 103.

10. G. K. Chesterton. *The Man Who Was Chesterton*. (Garden City, NY: Doubleday & Company, Inc., 1960), p. 106.

Chapter 8 - Logical Love

1. George MacDonald. *The Hope of the Gospel*. (London: Ward, Lock, Bowden and Co., 1892), p. 12.

2. Anders Nygren. *Agape and Eros*. (Philadelphia, PA: The Westminster Press, 1953), p. 131.

3. Cornelius J. Dyck, Ed. *An Introduction to Mennonite History*. (Scottdale, PA: Herald Press, 1967), p. 86.

4. Festo Kivengere. *I Love Idi Amin*. (Old Tappan, NJ: Fleming H. Revell Company, 1977), p. 63.

5. Ibid. p. 62.

6. Leo Tolstoy. *Last Diaries*. (NY: G.P. Putnam's Sons, 1960), p. 191.

7. The quotations in this paragraph are taken from an article on page 24 of the Marion, Indiana Chronicle-Tribune of January 16, 1978. Goldie Bristol describes this experience in a book published by Word Inc. in 1978 entitled *These Tears Are For Diane*.

8. E. Stanley Jones. *Christian Maturity*. (NY: Abington Press, 1957), p. 152.

9. Ibid. p. 153, 159.

10. Leo Tolstoy. *Resurrection*. (NY: Penguin Books, 1984), p. 450.

11. Thomas Merton. *Seeds of Contemplation*. (NY: Dell Publishing Company, Inc., 1949), p. 40.

12. C. S. Lewis. *The Weight of Glory*. (Grand Rapids, MI: Eerdmans Publishing, 1975), p. 14-15.

Chapter 9 - Love and Knowledge

1. Thomas Merton. *Seeds of Contemplation*. (NY: Dell Publishing Company, Inc., 1949), p. 14-15.

2. Alexis DeTocqueville, et al. *The Bitch-Goddess Success*. (NY: The Eakins Press, 1968), p. 23.

Chapter 10 - More Relationships

1. Guy F. Hershberger. *The Way of the Cross in Human Relations*. (Scottdale, PA: Herald Press, 1958), p. 312.

2. Alan Paton. *Cry. the Beloved Country*. (NY: Charles Scribner's Sons, 1948), p. XIX.

3. Thomas Merton. *No Man Is An Island*. (Garden City, NY: Doubleday & Company Inc., 1967), p. 133.

4. George MacDonald. *Creation in Christ*. (Wheaton, IL: Harold Shaw Publishers, 1976), p. 66f.

5. Fyodor Dostoevsky. *Crime and Punishment*. (Garden City, NY: International Collectors Library), p. 211.

6. Ibid. p. 10.

7. Norman L. Geisler. *The Christian Ethic of Love*. (Grand Rapids, MI: Zondervan Publishing House, 1973), p. 33.

8. Dostoevsky. p. 343.

9. C. S. Lewis. *The Abolition of Man*. (NY: Macmillan, 1968), pp. 52-53.

Part III - Obedience and Implications

Chapter 2 - Magic, Mirage, or Miracle

1. William Law. *A Serious Call to a Devout and Holy Life*. (Grand Rapids, MI: Baker Book House, 1977), p. 22.

2. William Barclay. *The Mind of St. Paul*. (London: Collins, 1958), p. 228.

Chapter 3 - Changed Lives

1. C. S. Lewis. *Mere Christianity*. (NY: The Macmillan Company, 1958), p. 157.
2. Ibid. p. 157.

Chapter 4 - Successful Superstar or Suffering Servant

1. George MacDonald. *What's Mine's Mine*. (London: Kegan, Paul, Trench, Trubner & Co. Ltd., 1900), p. 196.
2. Juan Carlos Ortiz. *Disciple*. (Carol Stream, IL: Creation House, 1975), p. 14.
3. Georges Gorree and Jean Barbier, Ed. *The Love of Christ*. (London: Fount Paperbacks, 1982), p. 56.
4. Ibid. p. 58.
5. Mother Teresa. *Words to Live By*. (Notre Dame, IN: Ave Marie Press, 1983), p. 73.
6. Gorree and Barbier. p. 59.

Chapter 5 - The Simple Life

1. This quotation and the rest of the incident are from the article, "Fat Cells in the Body: Issues of Loyalty" by Paul Brand with Philip Yancy in *Christianity Today*, Oct. 10, 1980.
2. Ibid.
3. The data in this paragraph came from the following book which uses such sources as the Organization for Economic Cooperation and Development and the U.S. Bureau of the Census, Abstract of the U.S. 1976. Ronald J. Sider. *Cry Justice*. (Downers Grove, IL: InterVarsity Press, 1980), pp. 60, 104, 159.
4. John V. Taylor. *Enough is Enough*. (Minneapolis, MN: Augsburg Publishing House, 1977, p. 20.
5. E. F. Schumacher. *Small is Beautiful*. (NY: Harper & Row, Publishers, 1973), p. 119.
6. Donald B. Kraybill. *The Upside-Down Kingdom*. (Scottdale, PA: Herald Press, 1978), p. 154.
7. Leo Tolstoy. *What Then Must We Do?* (London: Oxford

University Press, 1950), p. 194.

8. Schumacher. p. 57.

9. Ibid.

10. Vernard Eller. *The Simple Life.* (Grand Rapids, MI: Eerdmans Publishing Company, 1973), pp. 95-96.

11. Ibid. p. 114.

12. Ibid. p. 12.

13. Ronald J. Sider. *Living More Simply.* (Downers Grove, IL: InterVarsity Press, 1980), p. 12.

14. Georges Gorree and Jean Barbier. *Love Without Boundaries.* (Huntington, IN: Our Sunday Visitor, Inc., 1974), p. 62.

15. John Perkins. *With Justice for All.* (Ventura, CA: Regal Books, 1982), p. 107.

16. Eller. p. 122.

Chapter 6 - Community

1. Donald P. MacNeill, Douglas A. Morrison, and Henri J.M. Nouwen. *Compassion: A Reflection on the Christian Life.* (Garden City, NY: Image Books, 1983), p. 19.

2. Vance Packard. *A Nation of Strangers.* (NY: Simon & Schuster, 1982), p. 6.

3. Doris Janzen Longacre. *Living More With Less.* (Scottdale, PA: Herald Press, 1980), p. 33.

4. Ibid.

5. James J. Flick. *The Car Culture.* (Cambridge, MA: MIT Press, 1975), p. 176.

6. Gospel Evangel, April 1985. This is a publication of The Mennonite Church.

7. Eberhard Arnold. *God's Revolution.* (Ramsey, NJ: Paulist Press, 1984), pp. 129-130.

8. Ibid. p. 76.

9. Flick. p. 218.

10. *Marion Chronicle-Tribune.* Marion, IN. Jan. 25, 1981.

11. Flick. p. 218.

12. Robert S. Lynd and Helen Merrell Lynd. *Middletown.* (NY: Harcourt, Brace and Co., 1929), p. 65.

13. Flick. p. 161.

14. Marion Chronicle-Tribune. May 3, 1981.

15. Christianity Today, June 12, 1981, p. 29.

16. Time, Dec. 9, 1985, pp. 78-90.

17. Ibid.

18. Christianity Today, March 18, 1988, pp. 54-55.

19. Time.

20. Flick. p. 162.

21. George McRobie. *Small is Possible.* (NY: Harper and Row, 1981), p. 142.

22. James R. Newman. *Science and Sensibility.* (NY: Simon and Schuster, 1961), p. 457.

23. Virginia Stem Owens. *The Total Image.* (Grand Rapids, MI: Eerdmans, 1980, p. 66-67.

24. Francis A. Schaeffer. *No Little People.* (Downers Grove, IL: InterVarsity Press, 1974), p. 260.

25. Ibid. p. 261.

26. C.S. Lewis. *Mere Christianity.* (NY: Macmillan, 1958), p. 128.

Chapter 7 - Postulates, Paradoxes, and Pacifism

1. William Barclay. *The Gospel of Matthew*, Volume 1, Revised Edition. (Philadelphia, PA: The Westminster Press, 1975), p. 164.

2. Arthur F. Holmes, ed. *War and Christian Ethics.* (Grand Rapids, MI: Baker Book House, 1975), p. 49.

3. Roland H. Bainton. *Christian Attitudes Toward War and Peace.* (Nashville, TN: Abingdon Press, 1960), p. 78.

4. Ibid. p. 53-54, 67, 77.

5. John Howard Yoder. *Christian Attitudes to War, Peace, and Revolution: A Companion to Bainton.* (Elkhart, IN: Goshen Biblical Seminary, 1983), p. 307.

6. Ibid. p. 331.

7. <u>Ibid</u>. p. 317.

8. Arthur M. Eastman, General Editor. *The Norton Reader.* Third Edition. (New York: W.W. Norton & Company, Inc., 1973), p. 885.

9. Richard McSorley. *New Testament Basis of Peace Making.* (Scottdale, PA: Herald Press, 1985), p. 148.

10. Marion Chronicle-Tribune, May 27, 1988.